Shattered Syria
From Tyranny to Freedom

Table of Contents

Introduction 4
Chapter 1 The Rise of Tyranny 6
   The Birth of Dictatorship in Syria 7
   The Cult of Personality: Assad's Grip on Power 10
   Early Repression and the Seeds of Dissent 13
Chapter 2 The Spark of Revolution 16
   The Role of Social Media in Mobilization 17
   The Youth Uprising: The Beginning of Change 20
   Government Crackdowns and Escalating Violence ... 23
Chapter 3 Civil War Breaks Out 27
   The Descent into Chaos 28
   The Formation of Rebel Groups 31
   International Interventions: A Divided World 35
Chapter 4 The Humanitarian Crisis 39
   The Impact on Syrian Civilians 40
   Refugees and Displacement: The Exodus Begins 43
   The Strain on Neighboring Countries 47
Chapter 5 The War Within 52
   Factions and Fragmentation 53
   The Rise of Extremist Groups 57
   Power Struggles Among the Rebels 60
Chapter 6 The Role of International Powers 65

    Russia's Support for Assad 67

    The U.S. and the West: A Changing Strategy 70

    The Proxy War: Iran and the Middle East 74

Chapter 7 The Collapse of the State 78

    The Breakdown of Infrastructure 79

    The Disintegration of Government Control 83

    Lawlessness and the Rise of Militias 86

Chapter 8 The Struggle for Freedom 90

    The Call for Democracy and Human Rights 91

    The Syrian Opposition: A Fragmented Hope 94

    Women in the Revolution: Agents of Change 97

Chapter 9 The Global Response 102

    The Role of the United Nations 103

    Sanctions and Diplomatic Efforts 107

    Humanitarian Aid: The Lifeline for Syrians 110

Conclusion 114

Introduction

Shattered Syria: From Tyranny to Freedom is not just the story of a nation; it is the tale of resilience, suffering, and the enduring hope for freedom against the backdrop of oppression. For decades, Syria lived under the iron grip of the Assad regime, where tyranny was the status quo, and the people's voices were stifled by the weight of a dictatorship that controlled every facet of life. Yet, beneath the surface, the Syrian people carried an unyielding desire for freedom, justice, and a future free from fear.

In 2011, what began as a peaceful protest in the southern city of Daraa erupted into a full-scale revolution that would unravel the very fabric of the country. As the regime's violence escalated, the revolution evolved into a civil war—one that would drag Syria through an abyss of unimaginable suffering, destruction, and displacement. The cries for democracy turned into the sounds of artillery, the hopes for reform drowned out by bombs and gunfire.

This book takes you through the harrowing journey of Syria's descent into chaos. From the rise of the Assad family's tyrannical reign to the birth of a revolution that would engulf an entire nation, Shattered Syria explores the forces that have shaped the conflict. It dives deep into the complexities of a war that is not just fought by Syrians but also by global powers with competing interests. Yet, even in the midst of the devastation, Syria's people have shown an incredible resilience—fighting for the values of freedom and justice that once seemed out of reach.

Through these pages, we will examine the human cost of this war, the destruction of a proud nation, and the ongoing struggle for liberty and dignity. We will look at the sacrifices made, the lives lost, and the millions forced to flee their homes in search of safety and a new life.

But this story is also one of hope. Despite the brutalities, the atrocities, and the fractured landscape, Syria's journey is not yet over. The spirit of its people endures. This book is a reminder that freedom is worth fighting for—no matter the cost. The road to freedom is often long and painful, but in the end, the human desire for self-determination and dignity will always shine brighter than tyranny.

Shattered Syria is a tribute to those who have fought, bled, and died for a Syria they believe in—a Syria where the people are free, and their voices are no longer silenced.

Chapter 1
The Rise of Tyranny

Syria's descent into tyranny began long before the Assad regime took power, but it was with the rise of Hafez al-Assad in 1970 that the country would enter a new era of political repression and centralized control. After a series of coups and political instability in the 1960s, Hafez al-Assad, a military officer and member of the Alawite minority, seized power in a bloodless coup. His rise to prominence marked the beginning of a regime that would last for over four decades, with the Assad family transforming Syria into a one-party state under the control of the Ba'ath Party. The centralization of power, the suppression of political dissent, and the establishment of a cult of personality would become hallmarks of his rule, and later, his son Bashar al-Assad's reign.

Under Hafez al-Assad, Syria's political landscape was reshaped through a combination of fear, loyalty, and strategic alliances. The regime utilized the military, intelligence services, and an extensive network of patronage to consolidate power, stifling any opposition before it could gain traction. Political rivals were silenced, imprisoned, or eliminated, and the media was tightly controlled to ensure that only government-approved narratives reached the public. Despite the outward appearance of stability, the Syrian people were subjected to an environment of constant surveillance, censorship, and repression. Freedom of speech, political participation, and basic human rights were sacrificed at the altar of Assad's vision of unity and control.

When Hafez al-Assad passed away in 2000, his son Bashar al-Assad inherited a nation steeped in authoritarian rule. Bashar's ascent to power was heralded as a potential turning point—many believed he would bring reform to Syria and steer the country toward modernization. However, Bashar quickly adopted his father's style of leadership, demonstrating that his reign would be no different. The hopes for political change and economic improvement were soon dashed as the younger Assad further entrenched the regime's grip on power. Through violent crackdowns, the intimidation of dissidents, and the manipulation of sectarian divisions, Bashar's rise signaled that the brutal authoritarianism of the Assad family would continue to dominate Syrian life, preparing the ground for the explosion of frustration and anger that would ignite the revolution a decade later.

The Birth of Dictatorship in Syria

The roots of dictatorship in Syria stretch back to the early 20th century, during the period of colonial rule under the French Mandate. Syria, which had long been a crossroads for various empires and cultures, became a battleground for competing colonial powers. Following the collapse of the Ottoman Empire after World War I, the French took control of Syria in 1920, with the goal of establishing a puppet state under their influence. This colonial rule sparked widespread resentment among the Syrian population, who desired independence and self-determination. Yet, while the French imposed their authority, Syria remained a fractured society, with deeply embedded sectarian, ethnic, and political divisions. These divisions would lay the groundwork for the rise of authoritarianism in the decades to come.

After Syria gained its independence in 1946, the country struggled with political instability, frequent coups, and changing governments. The political environment in Syria was chaotic, marked by short-lived governments and the constant intervention of the military in national politics. By the early 1960s, Syria was caught in a cycle of military coups, each government struggling to find a lasting solution to the country's political fragmentation. The nation's leadership alternated between secular nationalists, pan-Arabists, and communists, but none could offer a solution to Syria's deep-rooted problems. The state was disjointed, often governed by military leaders who lacked legitimacy and could not build a coherent, unified political framework.

In this climate of instability, the rise of the Ba'ath Party in the 1960s provided the catalyst for a shift toward authoritarian rule. The Ba'ath Party, founded in the 1940s, advocated for Arab nationalism, socialism, and the unification of Arab countries. It sought to replace colonial influences with a strong Arab identity, uniting the Arab world under one banner. However, as the Ba'ath Party gained popularity, it became increasingly militarized. This process was especially visible in Syria, where the military played a central role in the country's politics. As Syria's political structure began to solidify under the Ba'ath, the military became the driving force behind the country's future.

The defining moment in Syria's transition to dictatorship came in 1970, when a young, ambitious military officer named Hafez al-Assad seized power in a bloodless coup. Hafez, who was a member of the Alawite minority, a sect of Shia Islam, managed to capitalize on the instability and infighting within the Ba'ath Party. He quickly positioned himself as the dominant figure in Syrian politics, consolidating his power by establishing control over the army and intelligence services. His coup, which is often referred to as the "Corrective Movement," was marked by a swift removal of his rivals within the party and the military. This marked the beginning of the Assad family's reign in Syria, one that would last for over four decades and set the stage for the totalitarian regime that would emerge.

Under Hafez al-Assad's leadership, the core characteristics of Syria's dictatorship took shape. The regime established a tightly controlled political system, with the Ba'ath Party at its helm, but the true power resided in the hands of the Assad family. Hafez used the military and intelligence agencies to enforce his rule, silencing opposition, suppressing political dissent, and ensuring that the regime's authority was never questioned. He built a pervasive system of patronage, rewarding loyalists with positions of power, wealth, and influence. Through brutal crackdowns, mass imprisonments, and the elimination of any political competition, Assad solidified his rule and ensured the survival of a dictatorship that would span generations. His leadership marked the birth of a regime that was unyielding in its commitment to power, one that would shape Syria's political landscape for decades to come.

The birth of dictatorship in Syria was not merely the creation of a family-run regime but the manifestation of deeper societal and political fractures. The Assad regime capitalized on these divisions, employing a strategy of divide and conquer to ensure its dominance. Through a combination of fear, repression, and strategic alliances, Hafez al-Assad created a totalitarian state where dissent was met with swift and violent retribution. His rule became synonymous with tyranny, and the foundation for Syria's future under the Assad family was firmly set in place.

The Cult of Personality: Assad's Grip on Power

The concept of a "cult of personality" is not new in authoritarian regimes, but the Assad family's establishment and maintenance of such a cult in Syria became a cornerstone of their long-lasting grip on power. Under Hafez al-Assad, the regime skillfully crafted an image of the leader as an almost divine figure, one whose wisdom, strength, and vision were irreplaceable. This cult of personality became the bedrock upon which Assad's totalitarian state was built, reinforcing his control over every aspect of Syrian life, and later shaping the way his son, Bashar al-Assad, would inherit the mantle of leadership.

From the moment Hafez al-Assad seized power in 1970, he began to consolidate control by creating a highly centralized political system in which his image permeated every facet of the Syrian state. The regime worked tirelessly to cultivate the perception that Assad was not just a political leader but a savior and protector of the Syrian people. His leadership was portrayed as essential for the survival of Syria itself, and any threat to his rule was equated with a threat to national unity and identity. The state's institutions, from the military to the media, were co-opted to perpetuate this message, and over time, the idea that Syria could not function without Hafez al-Assad became deeply ingrained in the national psyche.

A critical element in Assad's creation of a cult of personality was the state-controlled media, which played a pivotal role in shaping the public's perception of him. Newspapers, television broadcasts, and radio programs were all tightly regulated to ensure that only government-approved narratives were circulated. Hafez al-Assad's speeches were broadcast regularly, often with accompanying visuals that glorified his leadership. The portrayal of Assad as a protector and father of the nation became a constant theme, with messages of his infallibility and unparalleled wisdom reaching the public. His image appeared everywhere—on billboards, street murals, textbooks, and even in private homes. Citizens were expected to display portraits of the leader in their homes, symbolizing both loyalty and reverence.

The regime also utilized the concept of "Asadism" to cultivate loyalty to the state and its leader. Asadism became a political and social ideology that emphasized unity, stability, and devotion to the Assad family. It was deeply rooted in the narrative of Syria's modernization under Hafez al-Assad's leadership, even though much of the progress was illusory and often came at the cost of personal freedoms. This ideology further deepened the loyalty to Assad, particularly among his supporters in the military and the Alawite community, from which the Assad family hailed. The regime's use of sectarianism played a key role in maintaining this loyalty; the Assad family's Alawite heritage was often presented as an essential part of Syria's identity, with the regime positioning itself as the protector of minority groups in a largely Sunni-majority country.

Moreover, Hafez al-Assad's leadership was marked by a combination of ruthless repression and carefully calculated gestures of benevolence, which helped him maintain popular support among the masses. His regime offered tangible benefits to certain segments of society, particularly in urban areas, in exchange for their loyalty. Economic programs, limited social benefits, and selective opportunities for career advancement created a sense of dependence on the regime. While the system was inherently authoritarian, these gestures helped mitigate some of the resentment against his rule, ensuring that even those who felt oppressed by the regime were, to some extent, co-opted into its machinery.

The role of the military in perpetuating the Assad regime's cult of personality cannot be overstated. Under Hafez al-Assad, the military became not only a tool of oppression but also an instrument for cultivating loyalty to the leader. Officers and soldiers were indoctrinated into a system where their allegiance to Assad was paramount, and those who were loyal to him were rewarded with positions of power and privilege. Military parades and public celebrations of Assad's achievements further cemented his status as the figurehead of Syrian identity and success.

Upon Hafez al-Assad's death in 2000, his son, Bashar al-Assad, inherited this deeply entrenched cult of personality. While Bashar initially appeared as a potential reformist, he quickly adopted his father's methods, using the established machinery of state control to project his own image as the natural successor to his father's legacy. The transition from father to son was framed as the continuation of a sacred dynasty, and Bashar was presented as the next incarnation of Hafez's leadership—intelligent, visionary, and capable of leading Syria through the modern age. Even as Syria's problems deepened under his rule, Bashar continued to be depicted as a figure of strength and resilience, albeit with more modern media tools to maintain this illusion.

In the end, the cult of personality built around the Assad family was a critical factor in ensuring their survival. By positioning themselves as indispensable to the Syrian state and its very identity, the Assad regime turned Syria into a country where loyalty to the leader became synonymous with loyalty to the nation. The consequences of this deeply entrenched ideology are still felt today, as Syria grapples with the legacy of one of the most enduring and repressive dictatorships in the modern Middle East.

Early Repression and the Seeds of Dissent

The rise of Hafez al-Assad in 1970 marked the beginning of a new era in Syria, one where political dissent was systematically crushed, and opposition was not tolerated. His consolidation of power created a deeply repressive regime, one that controlled every aspect of Syrian life. The state's control over the military, media, and political institutions became the cornerstone of the Assad family's rule. In the early years of Assad's reign, he relied heavily on the security apparatus—intelligence agencies and military police—to ensure that his regime faced no significant opposition. These agencies became powerful tools for repression, enabling Assad to silence potential challengers both within the government and from outside it.

The early years of Assad's rule were marked by a brutal crackdown on political opponents and dissidents. Any person or group that questioned the legitimacy of the regime was swiftly targeted. Prominent political figures from the previous regimes, particularly members of rival factions, were either imprisoned, exiled, or executed. This included members of the Ba'ath Party itself, who had initially supported Assad's rise to power but later became targets once they were perceived as potential threats. Assad's regime used torture, imprisonment, and extra-judicial killings to instill fear and maintain control, ensuring that any attempt to challenge the status quo would be met with swift and violent retribution.

The initial years of repression created a climate of fear in Syria, where people learned to stay silent in the face of injustice. Dissent, whether political, social, or intellectual, was a dangerous game. The Assad regime's intelligence network was pervasive, with informants in every sector of society, ensuring that any form of resistance or opposition would be discovered and eradicated before it could spread. Universities, workplaces, and even private homes became sites of surveillance. People lived in constant fear that speaking out or organizing against the regime would lead to arrest, torture, or death. This created an atmosphere where the regime's control over the populace was absolute, and any form of opposition was effectively suffocated before it could take root.

However, despite this environment of intense repression, the seeds of dissent were slowly planted. The first major signs of discontent with Assad's rule appeared in the late 1970s and early 1980s, as the regime's unrelenting control began to strain Syria's social fabric. As Syria's population grew and educated youth began to demand more freedoms, the regime's heavy-handed tactics began to alienate segments of society. In 1976, as the regime's military involvement in Lebanon increased, the growing cost of this foreign intervention caused frustration among Syrians. Many felt that Syria's involvement in Lebanon, especially its intervention in the Lebanese Civil War, was damaging to the country's interests. The economic burden of this war and the sense of political stagnation led to dissatisfaction, especially among the urban middle class and intellectuals who had hoped for some form of liberalization under Assad's leadership.

The most significant flashpoint of early dissent came in 1982 with the massacre in Hama, which would go down as a grim reminder of the brutal tactics employed by the regime to crush any form of rebellion. The city of Hama, which had been a center of opposition to the regime, became the focus of one of the most infamous operations in Syria's modern history. The Muslim Brotherhood, a powerful Islamist organization that had been calling for an end to Assad's rule, staged an uprising in Hama. The regime, in turn, responded with overwhelming force, sending in the military to crush the revolt. The city was bombarded, and thousands of civilians were killed in the ensuing massacre. This event not only underscored the regime's ruthlessness but also sent a clear message to any potential opponents: dissent would not be tolerated under any circumstances.

While Assad's regime was able to quash these early attempts at resistance through violence, the seeds of dissent had already been sown. The repression and brutality faced by the Syrian people during this time created deep scars within society, and a growing sense of injustice began to take root. The massacres, the arrests, and the disappearances that became commonplace under Assad's rule began to fuel anger, particularly among the younger generations who had grown up under a regime that promised stability but delivered nothing but fear and suffering. This growing sense of disillusionment would, over time, manifest in the 2011 revolution, as the Syrian people, tired of the years of repression, would once again rise up against the Assad regime. The events of the early years of the Assad regime laid the groundwork for the long-simmering resentment that would eventually explode into open rebellion.

Chapter 2
The Spark of Revolution

The year 2011 marked a turning point in the history of Syria, as the winds of change sweeping across the Arab world ignited a spark of revolution within the country. The Arab Spring, a wave of protests and uprisings against long-standing autocratic regimes, had already engulfed Tunisia, Egypt, Libya, and Yemen. For years, the Syrian population had quietly endured repression, economic hardship, and limited freedoms under the Assad regime. However, the events unfolding in neighboring countries gave Syrians a renewed sense of hope that they, too, could challenge the entrenched dictatorship that had ruled them for decades. What began as small, localized protests would rapidly evolve into a national movement, driven by the collective frustration of a people tired of being oppressed.

The initial spark for Syria's revolution came from the southern city of Daraa, where a group of teenagers were arrested and tortured for writing anti-government graffiti on a school wall in March 2011. The simple act of defying the regime in such a public manner, however minor it seemed, triggered an outpouring of outrage across the country. News of the children's brutal treatment spread quickly, prompting widespread protests in Daraa demanding their release and calling for political reform. In response, the regime's forces cracked down violently, opening fire on the demonstrators and sparking further unrest. This brutal retaliation was not an isolated incident but a clear sign of the regime's determination to hold on to power at all costs. As the government's response grew increasingly violent, the protests spread to other cities, including Damascus and Aleppo, with people from all walks of life joining the calls for change.

What began as a demand for reforms soon transformed into an all-out rebellion against Assad's rule. Syrians were no longer just calling for the release of detained children or the lifting of censorship, but for an end to decades of autocracy and brutality. The regime's refusal to engage in meaningful dialogue with the protesters only deepened the divide between the government and the people. The protests quickly turned into clashes as security forces and military personnel were deployed to quell the growing unrest. As the violence escalated, so too did the resolve of the people. The repression only fueled the anger of the protesters, many of whom now saw the regime not as a government to be reformed, but as a regime to be overthrown. The spark that had ignited in Daraa was now a wildfire spreading across the nation, signaling the beginning of a revolution that would change the course of Syria's history forever.

The Role of Social Media in Mobilization

The role of social media in the Syrian revolution of 2011 cannot be overstated. As the Assad regime's violent repression of peaceful protests began to escalate, social media platforms became powerful tools for organizing, mobilizing, and spreading information among Syrians, both inside and outside the country. In a state where traditional forms of communication were heavily censored and the media was tightly controlled by the regime, social media emerged as a lifeline for Syrians seeking to express their grievances, organize protests, and document the atrocities being committed by government forces. These platforms offered an unprecedented opportunity to bypass state censorship, share real-time updates, and create a global conversation about Syria's struggle for freedom.

In the early stages of the revolution, social media platforms such as Facebook, Twitter, and YouTube became essential tools for protesters. They provided a space for activists and ordinary citizens to organize protests, spread calls for action, and gather support. Facebook, in particular, became a virtual meeting ground for activists, as well as a space for Syrians to share their stories and experiences. Activists would use Facebook groups to call for demonstrations, while photos, videos, and news reports would be shared in real-time, giving a voice to those on the ground. These social media platforms not only helped people stay informed about the rapidly changing situation but also allowed them to coordinate efforts, mobilizing protesters in different cities and towns to come together.

One of the most significant aspects of social media during the Syrian revolution was its role in documenting human rights abuses and exposing the brutality of the Assad regime. As the government cracked down on protests with increasing force, activists used their mobile phones and cameras to capture images and videos of the violence. Videos of peaceful protesters being shot, detained, or tortured quickly spread across social media platforms. These images and videos had a powerful effect, both on domestic and international audiences. For Syrians, seeing these visuals reinforced the reality of their shared struggle, while for the international community, it made the atrocities undeniable. The ability to share real-time footage brought the violence and repression into the global spotlight, creating pressure on foreign governments and international organizations to respond.

Moreover, social media allowed for the creation of a global network of solidarity. As Syrians continued to risk their lives by protesting on the streets, individuals and organizations from around the world were able to show their support via social media, raising awareness and organizing campaigns. Activists used Twitter to raise awareness of specific events, such as the arrest or killing of prominent figures, while hashtags like #FreeSyria and #SyriaRevolution became symbols of solidarity and global calls for action. The international response was often limited to diplomatic rhetoric, but the online campaign helped put the plight of Syrians on the global agenda, ensuring that the world could not turn a blind eye to the unfolding crisis. Social media also provided a platform for Syrian diaspora communities, who played a crucial role in amplifying the voices of those inside Syria and organizing international protests and fundraisers.

However, while social media proved to be a powerful tool for mobilization, it also carried significant risks. The Assad regime quickly adapted to the digital revolution, using the very platforms that activists relied on to track, monitor, and arrest dissenters. Surveillance tactics were employed to infiltrate online networks, and the regime would often track activists' social media activity, arresting those who were identified as key organizers or supporters of the protests. In some cases, social media accounts were hacked, and activists were coerced into revealing their sources or identities. Despite the risks, the role of social media in the revolution cannot be understated. It allowed Syrians to connect with each other, share vital information, and gain international attention in ways that were previously unimaginable under an authoritarian regime.

Social media also helped amplify the voices of Syria's diverse opposition groups. With a fragmented opposition lacking a unified front, social media helped bring together different factions of the revolution, creating a common space for them to coordinate efforts, share ideas, and push for change. Although there were deep ideological divisions within the opposition, social media provided a platform where individuals could unite behind the common goal of ending Assad's rule. While the revolution eventually fragmented into multiple factions, with varying objectives and priorities, social media ensured that the desire for freedom, democracy, and dignity was continuously visible, both within Syria and to the outside world.

In conclusion, social media played an indispensable role in the Syrian revolution by empowering ordinary people, amplifying the voices of dissent, and challenging the narrative that the Assad regime sought to control. It allowed Syrians to bypass censorship, organize protests, document human rights abuses, and create a global solidarity movement. Despite the challenges and risks involved, social media became a lifeline for those seeking to challenge an oppressive regime, and its role in the revolution was crucial in ensuring that the world bore witness to the struggle of the Syrian people for freedom.

The Youth Uprising: The Beginning of Change

The Syrian revolution of 2011 was not just a movement for political change; it was also a generational uprising led by the youth of Syria. For decades, the Assad regime had controlled the political landscape, silencing opposition and stifling any forms of dissent. Yet, beneath the surface, a new generation had grown up in an increasingly globalized world, exposed to ideas of freedom, democracy, and civil rights through the Internet and social media. By the time the revolution began, the youth of Syria were ready to challenge the old order and fight for their future.

The spark for Syria's revolution can be traced back to the actions of a small group of teenagers in the southern city of Daraa. In March 2011, several young boys spray-painted anti-government slogans on the walls of their school. The slogans were simple yet powerful: "The people want to bring down the regime." These words echoed the sentiments of millions of Syrians who were disillusioned with the Assad regime's authoritarian rule and its tight grip on power. The boys were arrested and tortured by the regime's security forces, an act that would later become a catalyst for mass protests. The brutality with which the regime responded to the children's simple act of defiance was met with outrage across the country, and it was the youth—particularly students and young professionals—who took the lead in organizing protests in solidarity with the victims.

The youth of Syria had long been dissatisfied with the oppressive regime, but the events in Daraa provided them with a rallying point. They had grown up under the shadow of the Assad regime, where political freedom was limited, the economy stagnated, and corruption was rampant. Many young Syrians felt a profound sense of hopelessness regarding their future. Jobs were scarce, educational opportunities were limited, and the regime's control over every aspect of life made it nearly impossible to make meaningful changes. For these young people, the revolution represented a chance to reshape their country, to fight for a future where their voices would no longer be silenced.

As protests began in Daraa and spread to other cities, it was clear that the youth were the driving force behind the revolution. Students, university graduates, and young professionals took to the streets, calling for the release of political prisoners, greater freedoms, and an end to the regime's corruption. They were joined by ordinary Syrians who had grown tired of the oppression, but it was the youth who provided the energy, the ideas, and the willingness to risk everything for change. The demands for reform quickly escalated into demands for the downfall of the regime itself. What started as a peaceful call for political freedoms became an all-out rebellion against the autocratic rule of the Assad family.

The youth uprising was marked by its creativity, energy, and determination. Young Syrians used social media to organize protests, share information, and expose the regime's brutality. Facebook, Twitter, and YouTube became tools for spreading the word, documenting the violence, and building a global movement of solidarity. Activists and young leaders, many of whom had no prior experience in politics, became the faces of the revolution. They worked tirelessly to organize protests, distribute pamphlets, and coordinate efforts between cities. Their use of technology allowed them to circumvent government censorship, providing a platform for Syrians to voice their opposition to the regime.

However, the regime's response to the youth-led uprising was swift and brutal. The peaceful protests were met with violent crackdowns, with security forces using live ammunition, tear gas, and even snipers to disperse crowds. Despite the violence, the youth remained resilient. They continued to protest, despite the risk of imprisonment, torture, and death. This unwavering determination to challenge the regime, despite the heavy cost, marked the youth uprising as a pivotal moment in Syria's history. The regime's brutality only strengthened the resolve of the young revolutionaries, who believed that their fight for change was not just a political struggle, but a moral one.

As the months went by and the violence escalated, the youth were joined by a diverse coalition of Syrians, including the middle class, intellectuals, and marginalized groups. However, it was the youth who had ignited the revolution, setting in motion a movement that would change Syria forever. Their energy, creativity, and sense of purpose were a direct challenge to the decades of repression that had defined the Assad regime. While the revolution ultimately led to a devastating civil war, the youth uprising represented the beginning of a profound shift in Syria's political and social landscape. It was a moment when a generation that had been silenced for so long finally found its voice, demanding a future defined by freedom, justice, and dignity.

The youth uprising of 2011, though ultimately crushed by the regime's military might, remains an indelible part of Syria's story. It marked the beginning of a long struggle for freedom, one that would continue in various forms over the following years. For the youth of Syria, it was not just a battle for political change but a fight for a future where they could live free from the shadow of tyranny. Their bravery and resilience continue to inspire those who continue to resist the Assad regime and seek a better future for Syria.

Government Crackdowns and Escalating Violence

As the Syrian revolution of 2011 began to gain momentum, the Assad regime's response was swift, violent, and uncompromising. The peaceful protests, which initially called for modest reforms, quickly escalated into a nationwide uprising demanding the downfall of the regime. In the face of mounting public pressure and growing demonstrations, the Assad government resorted to extreme measures, using its military and security forces to crush dissent through brutal crackdowns. What began as the repression of peaceful protests in cities like Daraa and Damascus rapidly escalated into widespread violence across the country, as the regime sought to maintain its grip on power at any cost.

The first significant sign of the regime's violent response came in March 2011, in Daraa, a small city in southern Syria. After several teenagers were arrested and tortured for writing anti-government graffiti, local protests erupted, demanding their release and calling for political reform. In an attempt to intimidate and deter further dissent, government forces opened fire on the demonstrators, killing several people. This marked the beginning of the regime's widespread use of force to quash the revolution. Instead of listening to the demands of the protesters, the Assad government doubled down on repression, dismissing the protesters as "terrorists" and "foreign agents" trying to destabilize the country. The government's violent tactics spread quickly to other cities, as protests flared up in the capital, Damascus, and in Aleppo, Syria's largest city.

The government's strategy involved the deployment of the military, the police, and various intelligence agencies to violently suppress demonstrations. Security forces used live ammunition, tear gas, rubber bullets, and even snipers to break up crowds. Peaceful protesters, including children, women, and the elderly, were killed in these brutal crackdowns. The regime sought to create an atmosphere of fear, sending a clear message to the Syrian people that any form of opposition, no matter how small, would be met with violent retribution. The government also engaged in large-scale arrests, detaining thousands of activists, protesters, and ordinary citizens who were suspected of supporting the revolution. These detainees were subjected to torture, forced confessions, and degrading treatment in Syrian prisons.

As the protests continued to grow, the regime's violence escalated. By the summer of 2011, it became clear that the government was willing to stop at nothing to maintain its power. The Assad regime began using heavy artillery, tanks, and helicopters to bombard protestors in cities such as Homs and Latakia. Entire neighborhoods were destroyed as the military ramped up its efforts to silence any opposition. The once-peaceful uprising quickly morphed into an armed conflict, with both the regime and the increasingly militarized opposition engaged in violent clashes. The government's crackdown was characterized by extrajudicial killings, massacres, and widespread human rights violations, including the use of chemical weapons against civilians, a tactic that would later become one of the regime's most notorious methods of repression.

The regime also relied on its extensive network of intelligence agencies to track and eliminate opposition figures. The feared Mukhabarat, or secret police, were tasked with identifying activists, opposition leaders, and anyone suspected of being involved in the revolution. These intelligence agencies used widespread surveillance, tapping into phone calls, emails, and social media accounts, to monitor and target individuals. The regime's brutal tactics extended to civilian neighborhoods, where residents were subjected to random raids, mass arrests, and collective punishment for their perceived support of the opposition. Entire villages and towns were placed under siege, with food, water, and medical supplies withheld in an effort to break the spirit of resistance.

One of the most infamous examples of government violence during this period occurred in the city of Hama in February 2012. The government's response to the protests in Hama, which had been a hotbed of dissent, was shockingly brutal. Security forces surrounded the city and unleashed a savage bombardment, targeting civilian homes and infrastructure. The violence resulted in hundreds of deaths, with estimates ranging from several hundred to over a thousand. This massacre not only highlighted the regime's willingness to use extreme force to suppress the revolution but also marked a turning point, where peaceful protests gave way to a brutal, full-scale civil war.

The violent government crackdowns and the escalating violence transformed the conflict into something far more complex than a simple revolution. The Assad regime's heavy-handed tactics alienated many Syrians who had initially called for reform, pushing some to take up arms in self-defense or to support rebel groups. The violence and repression from the government also led to the fragmentation of the opposition, with moderate factions struggling to hold their ground against radical groups and extremists who seized upon the chaos to further their agendas.

In the end, the Assad regime's violent suppression of dissent not only prolonged the conflict but also exacerbated the suffering of the Syrian people. It transformed what was once a struggle for political reform into a brutal civil war, characterized by widespread atrocities, forced displacement, and loss of life. The regime's unwillingness to negotiate or compromise ensured that the violence would escalate, pushing Syria deeper into a state of chaos and despair. The government's crackdown not only failed to quell the revolution, but it also deepened the divisions in Syrian society and fueled a cycle of violence that continues to affect the country to this day.

Chapter 3
Civil War Breaks Out

By the summer of 2011, the peaceful protests that had erupted in Syria in response to the brutal repression of demonstrators had transformed into full-scale armed resistance. The Assad regime's violent crackdown had not succeeded in quelling the growing movement for change; instead, it had pushed many disillusioned Syrians, including former protesters and defected soldiers, to take up arms. As security forces continued their brutal campaigns, including shelling civilian neighborhoods and arresting thousands of activists, the resistance began to take on a more militarized form. This shift marked the point at which what started as a popular uprising for reform morphed into a civil war, with Syria plunged into a protracted and devastating conflict.

The opposition groups in Syria were initially disorganized and fragmented, composed of defected soldiers, armed civilians, and dissidents who were united more by their opposition to Assad than by any coherent strategy or ideology. The first major rebel group to emerge was the Free Syrian Army (FSA), founded by defected military officers who had grown disillusioned with the Assad regime's tactics. The FSA quickly gained momentum as it sought to challenge the military's dominance and to protect the civilian population from the regime's brutal assaults. However, as the conflict escalated, the FSA was joined by an increasing number of smaller militias, many of which had different political or sectarian agendas. This fragmentation within the opposition made it difficult to unify against the Assad regime, while also creating an environment ripe for extremism to take root.

The turning point came in 2012, when the fighting intensified and the war spread to more cities, including Aleppo and Damascus, Syria's two largest urban centers. The Assad regime's forces, which included the military, paramilitary groups, and foreign militias, launched all-out offensives to recapture rebel-held areas. The government's use of heavy artillery, airstrikes, and chemical weapons to suppress opposition fighters increasingly targeted civilian populations, further fueling the resistance. The brutal violence, especially in cities like Homs, Aleppo, and Idlib, turned what was initially a political struggle into an all-encompassing civil war. While the Assad regime still controlled large parts of Syria, the opposition's ability to hold territory, recruit fighters, and continue operations from rural strongholds marked the growing complexity and expansion of the conflict. By this stage, Syria was no longer just facing an internal uprising; it had become a battleground in which multiple factions fought for control, drawing in global powers and causing immense suffering for the Syrian people.

The Descent into Chaos

By 2013, the Syrian conflict had moved beyond a simple struggle for political change or reform and had descended into a full-blown civil war. The violence, which began with protests against the Assad regime, had now engulfed the entire nation, leaving a shattered landscape in its wake. As the war dragged on, the Syrian people found themselves trapped in a spiral of chaos that would claim countless lives, displace millions, and destabilize the entire region. What had begun as a demand for democratic reforms had evolved into a battle for survival, as the regime, opposition forces, and various external actors waged an increasingly brutal war, each with their own agendas.

The early years of the conflict saw the rise of various rebel groups, many of which were formed from defected soldiers and civilians who had taken up arms to fight against the Assad regime. However, as the war intensified, these groups began to fragment and splinter into increasingly diverse factions. Some rebel groups were motivated by a desire for democratic change, while others were driven by sectarian or ideological goals. This fragmentation created an environment where it became increasingly difficult to discern who was fighting whom, and why. Local militias, extremist groups like ISIS, and the Kurdish YPG (People's Defense Units) all vied for control of territory, complicating the battlefield and making any effort to unify the opposition nearly impossible. The lack of coordination and central leadership within the rebel factions allowed the regime to exploit the disarray, as it focused on isolating and eliminating weaker groups while strengthening its hold on key areas.

One of the key factors in the descent into chaos was the involvement of foreign powers. Early on, the Assad regime found critical support from its allies, most notably Russia and Iran, which provided military, financial, and logistical assistance. Russian airstrikes and Iranian-backed militias, particularly Hezbollah, gave the regime the necessary firepower to withstand the rebellion and to maintain control over major cities. On the other side, the opposition was also receiving external support, though it was more fragmented. The United States, Turkey, and several Gulf Arab countries provided funding, weapons, and training to various rebel factions, with the goal of ousting Assad and supporting a political transition. However, the lack of coordination between these international powers often meant that the aid they provided fueled internal rivalries and division within the opposition. The U.S.-backed Syrian Democratic Forces, composed primarily of Kurdish fighters, also found themselves at odds with both the Assad regime and other opposition factions. The introduction of competing foreign interests transformed Syria into a proxy battleground, where global powers were not only shaping the future of Syria but were also contributing to the further destabilization of the region.

As the war wore on, the scale of human suffering became almost unimaginable. The Assad regime's strategy of targeting civilian infrastructure—schools, hospitals, water supplies—had devastating effects on the population. The use of barrel bombs, chemical weapons, and starvation sieges became common tactics employed by the regime to break the will of the opposition. The United Nations and human rights organizations documented widespread atrocities, including mass executions, torture, and the use of chemical agents like sarin gas in attacks on civilian areas, most notably in the 2013 Ghouta attack. Meanwhile, rebel factions and extremist groups also committed their own atrocities, including the use of suicide bombings, indiscriminate attacks on civilians, and ethnic cleansing in areas under their control.

The humanitarian toll of the conflict was catastrophic. By 2014, more than 200,000 Syrians had lost their lives, and millions more had been displaced both internally and across borders. Neighboring countries such as Lebanon, Jordan, and Turkey bore the brunt of the refugee crisis, with millions of Syrians seeking asylum. The refugee exodus would grow into one of the largest humanitarian crises of the 21st century, further straining international resources and challenging the global community to respond effectively. The city of Aleppo, once a vibrant cultural hub, became a symbol of the war's destruction, with entire neighborhoods reduced to rubble, schools and hospitals destroyed, and basic necessities like food and medicine in short supply.

As Syria plunged deeper into chaos, the conflict also spread beyond its borders. The rise of ISIS in 2014 further complicated the situation, as the extremist group seized large portions of northern and eastern Syria, and later Iraq, creating a self-proclaimed caliphate. ISIS's brutal tactics, including mass executions, the destruction of cultural heritage sites, and the subjugation of religious and ethnic minorities, turned parts of Syria into a war zone like no other. The U.S.-led coalition, along with Kurdish forces, engaged in a bloody battle to reclaim ISIS-held territories, but the fight against the jihadist group only added to the region's instability.

The descent into chaos left Syria a broken nation. The political landscape became unrecognizable, with multiple competing factions, foreign powers, and extremist groups all fighting for control. The war turned Syria into a land of destruction, dislocation, and devastation, with no clear end in sight. The initial hopes for democratic change were replaced by a grim reality where survival was the primary concern for millions of Syrians. The war also reshaped the Middle East, creating long-lasting repercussions for regional stability and global geopolitics. The cost of the war, in terms of both human lives and regional security, continues to reverberate to this day.

The Formation of Rebel Groups

As the Syrian uprising transitioned from peaceful protests to an armed struggle against the Assad regime, various groups began to form within the opposition, each with its own agenda, ideology, and strategy. The formation of these rebel groups was a natural consequence of the Assad regime's brutal crackdown on demonstrators, which left many Syrians with no choice but to take up arms in self-defense. What started as a spontaneous outpouring of anger and frustration quickly morphed into a fragmented and increasingly militarized resistance movement. This led to the creation of numerous rebel groups, each with its own vision for Syria's future, making the opposition movement not only diverse but also highly fragmented.

The first significant rebel formation was the Free Syrian Army (FSA), which emerged in July 2011. The FSA was primarily composed of defected Syrian soldiers who had turned against the regime. These defectors, led by Colonel Riad al-Asaad, formed the backbone of the early opposition. Their goal was to create a military force capable of fighting the Assad regime and protecting civilians. The FSA was initially viewed as a unifying force, composed of a broad spectrum of Syrians who were united in their opposition to Assad's brutal tactics. The group's military tactics focused on guerrilla warfare, ambushes, and small-scale attacks aimed at weakening the regime's control over various territories. The FSA received some support from Western powers, including weapons and training, though this support was inconsistent and fragmented. Despite early successes, the FSA struggled with issues of cohesion and leadership. With no centralized command structure, the FSA became susceptible to fragmentation as various local commanders gained control of different territories, often pursuing their own agendas.

The rise of the FSA also marked the beginning of the proliferation of smaller, local militias. As the war progressed, these groups became more prominent and played an increasingly important role in the conflict. Many of these militias were formed along sectarian lines, which further complicated the situation. Some of the most prominent of these groups were local militias that formed in response to the regime's attacks on specific communities. These included Jabhat al-

Nusra, which emerged in 2012 as the Syrian branch of al-Qaeda, and Ahrar al-Sham, an Islamist group with significant support in the opposition areas. These groups, while fighting for the same goal—to overthrow Assad—often differed drastically in their methods and ideologies, ranging from secular groups like the FSA to more radical Islamist factions like Jabhat al-Nusra.

As the war escalated, the opposition saw the rise of even more extremist and radical factions. The Islamic State of Iraq and Syria (ISIS), or Daesh, became the most notorious of these groups. Originally a branch of al-Qaeda, ISIS exploited the chaos of the civil war to gain control over vast swathes of territory in both Syria and Iraq, proclaiming the creation of a self-declared caliphate in 2014. Their brutal methods, including mass executions, torture, and the destruction of cultural landmarks, shocked the world. ISIS, unlike other rebel factions, sought to impose its strict interpretation of Islamic law and had no interest in cooperating with other opposition groups, including secular and moderate factions. The rise of ISIS further complicated the already fragmented opposition, creating a rift among the rebel groups and leaving many to fight not only Assad but also the growing threat of extremism within their ranks.

On the other hand, the Syrian Democratic Forces (SDF), a Kurdish-led alliance of fighters, emerged as a powerful force in the fight against both the Assad regime and ISIS. The SDF, which included Syrian Kurds, Arabs, and Assyrians, was primarily composed of the People's Defense Units (YPG), a Kurdish militia. The Kurds, who had long been marginalized by the Syrian government, saw the civil war as an opportunity to carve out an autonomous region in northern Syria, known as Rojava. The YPG and its allies received significant support from the U.S.-led coalition in the fight against ISIS, and they managed to seize large parts of northern Syria, including the strategic city of Kobani. However, the SDF's focus on creating an autonomous Kurdish region put them at odds with both the Syrian government and Turkey, which viewed Kurdish separatism as a threat to its own territorial integrity.

The proliferation of rebel groups also led to the rise of foreign-backed militias. Countries such as Saudi Arabia, Qatar, and Turkey provided varying levels of support to different factions within the opposition. Saudi Arabia and Qatar generally backed more Islamist rebel groups, such as Ahrar al-Sham and Jaish al-Islam, while Turkey provided substantial support to groups with a focus on defeating both Assad and the Kurdish forces. These foreign interventions further fueled the fragmentation of the opposition and complicated efforts to create a unified front against Assad. As a result, the war became more of a proxy conflict, with external powers backing their preferred factions, each with their own set of interests in Syria's future.

In conclusion, the formation of rebel groups in Syria was a direct response to the brutal suppression of peaceful protests by the Assad regime. The lack of unity within the opposition and the varying ideological, sectarian, and external influences led to a fragmented and often disjointed resistance movement. While the initial goal was to overthrow the Assad regime and implement democratic reforms, the formation of radical Islamist factions, the rise of ISIS, and the involvement of foreign powers turned the war into a complex and bloody struggle for control. The lack of coordination and leadership among these rebel groups not only prolonged the war but also allowed the Assad regime to capitalize on the divisions within the opposition, ultimately contributing to the ongoing chaos and suffering in Syria.

International Interventions: A Divided World

The Syrian civil war, which began in 2011, quickly escalated from a domestic uprising against a brutal regime into a complex international conflict. As the Assad regime faced growing resistance, both from within Syria and from various rebel factions, foreign powers became heavily involved, each with their own strategic interests, alliances, and objectives. This foreign intervention not only shaped the course of the war but also polarized the international community, turning Syria into a battleground for global power struggles. The conflict, initially framed as a fight for freedom and democracy, soon became an arena where geopolitical considerations outweighed the original aspirations of the Syrian people.

From the outset of the revolution, the Assad regime found critical support from two key allies: Russia and Iran. Russia, under President Vladimir Putin, saw Syria as a crucial strategic partner in the Middle East, particularly as a counterbalance to U.S. influence in the region. Russia's military and diplomatic support was vital in keeping the Assad regime afloat. Moscow provided significant military aid, including weapons, intelligence, and, eventually, direct military intervention. In September 2015, Russia began conducting airstrikes in Syria, primarily targeting rebel groups opposed to Assad, as well as ISIS. Russian airpower was instrumental in reversing the fortunes of the Assad regime, allowing it to regain critical territories, including Aleppo. Furthermore, Russia used its veto power at the United Nations Security Council to block resolutions that called for sanctions against Assad, further emboldening the regime and extending the war.

Iran, on the other hand, has been a long-standing ally of the Assad regime, largely due to shared geopolitical and sectarian interests. As a Shia-majority country, Iran saw Assad's Alawite-led regime as an important regional ally in countering Sunni-majority forces and radical Islamists, especially in light of its own rivalries with Sunni-majority countries like Saudi Arabia. Iran's intervention in Syria was multifaceted: it provided financial support, military advisers, and weapons to the Assad regime, and it also sent in fighters from its elite military units, including the Quds Force of the Islamic Revolutionary Guard Corps (IRGC). In addition to Iranian forces, Hezbollah, the Lebanese militant group backed by Iran, also played a crucial role, providing ground troops and helping Assad's forces reclaim critical territories. This Iranian and Hezbollah involvement further deepened Syria's sectarian divide and transformed the conflict into a broader regional struggle between Sunni and Shia powers.

On the opposite side of the conflict, a coalition of Western and Arab states, including the United States, Turkey, Saudi Arabia, and Qatar, threw their support behind various opposition groups, though often with conflicting objectives. The U.S. initially supported the Syrian opposition with non-lethal aid, such as food, medicine, and training, but as the war progressed, the U.S. shifted its focus to fighting ISIS, a rising and brutal force in the region. The U.S. formed the International Coalition Against ISIS, providing airstrikes, weapons, and intelligence to local Kurdish and Arab forces, most notably the Syrian Democratic Forces (SDF). The U.S. also conducted direct airstrikes against Assad's forces when they were perceived as a threat to American-backed rebels or Kurdish forces. However, the U.S. was reluctant to fully intervene in Syria's civil war, and its support for opposition groups was inconsistent, further contributing to the fragmentation of the rebel forces.

Turkey played a particularly complex role in the conflict. Initially, Turkey supported the Syrian opposition, providing logistical support, weapons, and safe havens for rebel groups along its border with Syria. However, Turkey's primary concern became the growing influence of Kurdish forces, particularly the YPG (People's Defense Units), which it saw as an extension of the PKK (Kurdistan Workers' Party), a Kurdish separatist group fighting for autonomy in Turkey. In response, Turkey launched several military operations in northern Syria, aimed at preventing the establishment of a Kurdish autonomous region along its border, and directly confronting both ISIS and the Kurdish forces backed by the U.S. This involvement shifted Turkey's stance, leading to a complex set of alliances and confrontations with other international actors.

Saudi Arabia and Qatar, both key Sunni powers in the region, supported various Islamist rebel groups, including Ahrar al-Sham and Jaish al-Islam, in an effort to weaken the Assad regime and curb Iran's growing influence in Syria. Both countries, along with Turkey, were motivated by sectarian considerations, as they sought to counter the Shia-aligned forces backing Assad. Their support, which included funding, arms, and training for opposition fighters, exacerbated the fragmentation of the Syrian rebel movement, contributing to the rise of more radical factions within the opposition, including Jabhat al-Nusra (al-Qaeda's Syrian affiliate).

The conflicting interests of these international powers created a deeply divided world, with Syria serving as the focal point for competing geopolitical and ideological struggles. The Russian-Iranian alliance sought to preserve the status quo and support a long-standing regional ally, while the U.S.-led coalition aimed to counter the rise of ISIS and limit Iran's influence in the region. At the same time, regional powers like Turkey, Saudi Arabia, and Qatar pursued their own agendas, each acting in ways that complicated efforts for a unified, peaceful resolution to the conflict. This web of foreign interventions, with each power pursuing its own interests, has prolonged the war and made the prospects for a peaceful resolution seem increasingly remote.

In conclusion, the international interventions in Syria have turned the conflict into a proxy war, where global and regional powers have engaged in a struggle for influence, with little regard for the humanitarian suffering of the Syrian people. These interventions have not only prolonged the war but have also fragmented the opposition, empowered extremist factions, and worsened the humanitarian crisis. Syria's descent into chaos has become a tragic example of how foreign intervention, driven by competing interests, can turn a domestic conflict into a global disaster.

Chapter 4
The Humanitarian Crisis

As the Syrian civil war entered its second year, the conflict's human toll became increasingly apparent. What began as a political struggle for reform quickly spiraled into a devastating humanitarian crisis that would affect millions of Syrians. The war's brutal tactics—ranging from indiscriminate bombings to chemical weapon attacks—left deep scars on the civilian population. By the time international attention turned to the scale of the devastation, Syria had already become a shattered state, with entire communities displaced, children orphaned, and countless lives lost. The consequences of the conflict were felt not only within Syria's borders but also in neighbouring countries, which bore the brunt of the refugee crisis.

The Assad regime's use of heavy artillery, airstrikes, and chemical weapons on civilian populations exacerbated the humanitarian crisis, targeting hospitals, schools, and marketplaces in an attempt to break the spirit of resistance. The siege of entire cities, like Aleppo and Homs, became common as the regime sought to starve out opposition forces and their supporters. These military tactics, including the use of barrel bombs and chemical agents, aimed to terrorize civilians and force them into submission. As essential services collapsed, people were deprived of basic necessities such as food, clean water, medical care, and shelter. The deliberate targeting of civilian infrastructure and the use of siege tactics were clear violations of international law, yet they continued unchecked, leading to a growing death toll and widespread suffering.

The humanitarian toll of the Syrian conflict was not only seen in the death and destruction but also in the mass displacement of civilians. Millions of Syrians were forced to flee their homes, either internally or across international borders. The United Nations estimated that by 2015, more than 4 million Syrians had fled the country, with neighboring countries like Turkey, Lebanon, and Jordan hosting the largest numbers of refugees. Inside Syria, the displaced population grew to more than 7 million, many living in overcrowded refugee camps or makeshift shelters, struggling to survive in conditions of extreme poverty and uncertainty. The crisis also put a tremendous strain on the countries hosting refugees, leading to social, economic, and political challenges. The sheer scale of displacement added to the complexity of the conflict, as it was not just a battle between factions but a humanitarian emergency with profound global implications.

The Impact on Syrian Civilians

The Syrian civil war has had a profound and devastating impact on the civilian population, turning Syria into one of the largest humanitarian crises of the 21st century. What began as peaceful protests for political reform evolved into a brutal conflict that has left a lasting legacy of destruction, displacement, and suffering. Millions of Syrians have been affected by the violence, with many enduring physical, emotional, and psychological trauma. The war's toll on civilians is not just measured in lives lost, but also in the long-term effects it has had on the fabric of Syrian society.

One of the most immediate and visible impacts on Syrian civilians has been the widespread loss of life. From the early days of the conflict, government forces, including the military and intelligence agencies, used heavy artillery, airstrikes, and sniper fire to quell protests and combat opposition groups. Civilians who were not directly involved in the conflict were caught in the crossfire. Attacks on civilian infrastructure, such as hospitals, schools, and marketplaces, became common, as the Assad regime sought to punish communities perceived to be sympathetic to the rebels. These attacks often led to mass casualties, with entire families killed or wounded. In many cases, civilians were subjected to chemical weapon attacks, such as the 2013 chemical weapons attack in Ghouta, which killed hundreds of people, mostly women and children, and injured thousands more. These attacks marked a clear violation of international law and left the civilian population living in constant fear of indiscriminate violence.

Beyond the immediate toll of death and injury, the conflict has had a profound effect on the mental health of Syrians. The war's constant threat of violence, the loss of loved ones, and the destruction of homes have left deep psychological scars on the population. Many survivors of bombings, massacres, and chemical attacks have been left with lifelong physical disabilities, but the emotional toll has been equally devastating. PTSD, depression, and anxiety have become widespread, especially among children who have witnessed the horrors of war. Families torn apart by the conflict, the loss of a home, and the constant displacement have created a generation of Syrians struggling with trauma. For children, many of whom have known no life but war, the impact is even more severe, as the experience of living through violence and instability deprives them of a normal childhood and opportunities for education and emotional development.

Another devastating consequence for civilians has been the displacement crisis. Millions of Syrians have been forced to flee their homes, either internally within the country or across international borders. By 2015, over 4 million Syrians had fled the country, with the majority seeking refuge in neighboring countries such as Turkey, Lebanon, and Jordan. These countries, already struggling with their own social and economic challenges, have borne the brunt of the refugee crisis, with limited resources to accommodate the vast influx of displaced Syrians. Inside Syria, more than 7 million people were displaced, many living in makeshift camps or with relatives, struggling to survive in conditions of extreme poverty. The lack of access to basic services such as healthcare, education, and sanitation in these camps has further exacerbated the suffering of the displaced population. The situation for refugees and internally displaced persons (IDPs) has been marked by overcrowding, inadequate shelter, and lack of clean water and food, contributing to a heightened vulnerability to disease, malnutrition, and exploitation.

In addition to physical displacement, the war has fractured Syrian society in ways that will take decades to heal. The civil war has exacerbated existing sectarian and ethnic divisions, with various factions—Shia, Sunni, Alawite, Christian, Kurdish, and others—caught in the crossfire. The rise of extremist groups like ISIS has further fueled sectarian violence, leading to the displacement of entire communities based on their religious or ethnic identity. Thousands of Syrians have been subjected to forced migration due to their religion or ethnicity, while others have been targeted for their political beliefs. The war has also destroyed much of Syria's infrastructure, including its healthcare and educational systems, leaving a generation of young Syrians without access to education and medical care. The destruction of homes, schools, and hospitals has further disrupted normal life, making it difficult for many to rebuild their lives even after fleeing to safety.

The impact of the war on Syrian civilians is not just a matter of the immediate violence, but also the long-term consequences. The destruction of communities, the breakdown of social networks, and the loss of essential services have left deep wounds that will take generations to heal. Many Syrians who have fled the conflict have been left with uncertain futures, unable to return to their homeland due to ongoing violence and instability. The war has created a cycle of poverty, trauma, and displacement that will affect Syrian society for years to come, making the task of reconstruction and reconciliation all the more difficult.

In conclusion, the impact of the Syrian civil war on civilians has been catastrophic. The loss of life, displacement, psychological trauma, and destruction of infrastructure have created a nation in ruins. The consequences of the war will be felt by Syrians for generations to come, with lasting effects on their mental health, social fabric, and prospects for rebuilding. The international community's response to the crisis has been insufficient in addressing the needs of those affected, and Syria's recovery will require sustained efforts to support its people in overcoming the immense challenges they face.

Refugees and Displacement: The Exodus Begins

The Syrian civil war, which began in 2011, has resulted in one of the largest and most complex refugee crises in modern history. As the violence escalated and government forces targeted civilian areas, millions of Syrians were forced to flee their homes, seeking safety both within Syria and in neighboring countries. What began as an exodus from conflict zones quickly evolved into a mass displacement crisis, as families, communities, and entire cities were uprooted. The scale of the crisis, driven by the brutality of the regime's attacks and the growing power of extremist groups like ISIS, created an overwhelming wave of refugees that has had profound implications for the entire region and the world.

By the end of 2012, as the conflict intensified and government airstrikes, shelling, and ground operations became widespread, millions of Syrians began to leave their homes in search of safety. Initially, the majority of displaced Syrians sought refuge in nearby countries such as Lebanon, Turkey, and Jordan, which shared borders with Syria. These neighboring countries became the first line of defense, absorbing a large percentage of the refugee population. Turkey, in particular, set up refugee camps along its southern border, offering a temporary haven for those fleeing the violence. However, as the war dragged on, the number of refugees quickly outpaced the resources available in these countries, leading to overcrowded conditions and increasingly dire humanitarian needs.

Lebanon, a small country with its own political and economic challenges, became home to more than one million Syrian refugees by 2014—making up nearly a quarter of its population. The influx of refugees strained Lebanon's already fragile infrastructure, social services, and economy. Similarly, Jordan, which had long hosted Palestinian refugees, saw the number of Syrian refugees in its camps increase exponentially. The Zaatari refugee camp, located in northern Jordan, became one of the largest refugee camps in the world, housing over 100,000 Syrians by 2014. While neighboring countries were providing shelter, they were often ill-equipped to handle the overwhelming numbers, resulting in insufficient access to essential services like healthcare, education, and clean water. This led to worsening conditions for refugees, who lived in overcrowded camps with limited opportunities for work or integration into the host communities.

Inside Syria, millions of people became internally displaced persons (IDPs), fleeing from one part of the country to another in search of safety. Cities like Aleppo, Homs, and Hama became war zones, with entire neighborhoods reduced to rubble by airstrikes and artillery bombardments. As the regime continued its policy of targeting opposition-held areas and the conflict spread across the country, civilians were left with no choice but to leave their homes and move to other regions. The displacement within Syria exacerbated the humanitarian crisis, with many families living in makeshift shelters, camps, or with relatives. With no access to basic services, food, and medical care, these displaced populations were among the most vulnerable in the country.

By 2015, the crisis reached new heights, with more than 4 million Syrians having fled the country. The majority of these refugees were concentrated in Turkey, Lebanon, Jordan, Iraq, and Egypt, but others made dangerous journeys across the Mediterranean Sea to reach Europe. This mass migration triggered a global response, with European countries grappling with how to handle the influx of refugees. The European Union, initially hesitant to offer asylum to large numbers of Syrians, was eventually forced to negotiate agreements to share the burden of the refugee crisis. In 2015, the EU reached a deal with Turkey to stem the flow of refugees to Europe in exchange for financial support and a promise to resettle a certain number of Syrians within the EU. However, despite international efforts to address the refugee crisis, many Syrians faced dangerous journeys, harsh living conditions, and uncertain futures.

The journey itself was fraught with peril. Many Syrians, particularly those fleeing by sea, faced deadly risks in their bid to reach safety. Overcrowded boats, inadequate safety measures, and the ever-present threat of drowning made the Mediterranean crossing one of the most dangerous migration routes in the world. Refugees were often at the mercy of smugglers who charged exorbitant fees for passage and left them vulnerable to exploitation. Reports of refugees drowning, being trafficked, or suffering from dehydration and exhaustion were widespread, underscoring the harsh realities of fleeing war.

For the Syrians who managed to escape the immediate violence, life in exile remained fraught with difficulties. Refugees in neighboring countries lived in limbo, with few legal rights, limited employment opportunities, and little hope of returning home. Those who made it to Europe faced the challenge of integrating into new societies, often encountering anti-immigrant sentiment and a lack of social support. Although some European countries, such as Germany and Sweden, accepted large numbers of refugees, many others closed their borders or offered limited assistance, leaving refugees with few options for resettlement. The lack of a clear path to citizenship or permanent residency left many Syrians in a state of uncertainty, unable to fully rebuild their lives or contribute to the communities they had sought refuge in.

The displacement crisis has had lasting effects on both the refugees themselves and the countries hosting them. For the displaced Syrians, the trauma of leaving behind their homes, communities, and loved ones has been compounded by the difficulties of living as refugees. Children, in particular, have been hit hard, with millions missing out on education and growing up in refugee camps or conflict zones. Many refugees face significant mental health challenges, including PTSD, depression, and anxiety, due to their experiences of violence, loss, and displacement. The prolonged nature of the crisis, with no clear resolution in sight, has left Syrians living in a state of uncertainty and despair.

In conclusion, the exodus of Syrians from their war-torn country has been a direct result of the conflict's devastating impact on civilians. The mass displacement of millions of people has created a complex humanitarian crisis that continues to affect neighboring countries, the broader Middle East, and the international community. The refugee crisis has exposed the limitations of international aid and the inability of many countries to cope with the scale of displacement. As Syria remains in a state of instability, the journey of refugees and displaced persons continues, with no easy solutions on the horizon.

The Strain on Neighboring Countries

The Syrian civil war, which erupted in 2011, has had a profound and long-lasting impact not only on the Syrian people but also on the neighboring countries that have been forced to bear the brunt of the refugee crisis. As millions of Syrians fled their war-torn homeland, countries such as Turkey, Lebanon, Jordan, and Iraq found themselves grappling with the overwhelming challenge of providing shelter, food, healthcare, and basic services to large numbers of refugees. These neighboring nations, already facing their own economic and social challenges, were thrust into a humanitarian crisis of unprecedented proportions.

Turkey has been the largest host country for Syrian refugees, providing sanctuary to over 3.6 million Syrians by 2020. The sheer scale of this influx has strained Turkey's infrastructure, particularly in the border regions. The government set up numerous refugee camps, particularly in the southeastern part of the country, where many refugees found temporary shelter. However, as the war dragged on and the refugee population continued to grow, the camps became overcrowded, and living conditions deteriorated. Many refugees were forced to leave the camps and seek shelter in urban areas, where they faced difficulty finding adequate housing and employment. The presence of such a large refugee population also put pressure on local resources, such as healthcare, education, and public services. Turkey, already grappling with its own economic challenges, found it increasingly difficult to accommodate the large refugee population, and the cost of supporting these refugees became a significant burden on the country's economy.

Despite the challenges, Turkey's government has continued to provide asylum to the majority of Syrians fleeing the conflict, but tensions have risen over time. Many Syrian refugees have faced hostility and discrimination from parts of the Turkish population, particularly as the economic situation worsened and competition for jobs increased. Some segments of the Turkish public began to view the refugee population as a burden rather than a group in need of humanitarian aid. This growing resentment has at times led to social unrest and protests against the government's handling of the refugee crisis. Moreover, Turkey's political stance toward the refugees has also become a point of contention, as the Turkish government has used the refugee issue as leverage in negotiations with the European Union, particularly in securing financial aid and political support.

In Lebanon, the Syrian refugee crisis has been particularly acute due to the country's small size, fragile economy, and pre-existing sectarian tensions. By 2014, Lebanon had taken in over 1.1 million Syrian refugees, making it the country with the highest per capita refugee population in the world. The massive influx of refugees placed immense pressure on Lebanon's already strained infrastructure, healthcare system, and education sector. The Lebanese government struggled to provide adequate services for both refugees and the local population, leading to increased competition for limited resources. Refugees often lived in overcrowded, makeshift shelters or informal settlements, which lacked basic sanitation and clean water. The refugee crisis also exacerbated Lebanon's internal sectarian divisions, as the Sunni-majority refugee population was often seen as a source of tension within the predominantly Shia and Christian country. The strain on Lebanon's public services, such as electricity, water, and waste management, further contributed to the sense of frustration among both refugees and local citizens.

The Lebanese economy, already struggling with high levels of debt and political instability, faced further setbacks due to the refugee crisis. The influx of Syrians contributed to rising unemployment and economic stagnation, particularly in areas with a high concentration of refugees. Additionally, the burden on Lebanon's health and education systems became a serious challenge, as schools and hospitals were stretched beyond capacity. The international community provided some financial aid to Lebanon, but the country's political instability and weak governance structures meant that much of this aid did not reach those who needed it most. The long-term presence of such a large refugee population also raised concerns about the potential for permanent displacement, as many Syrians were unable to return to their homeland due to the ongoing violence and instability in Syria.

Jordan, another neighboring country, also faced enormous challenges in hosting Syrian refugees. By 2015, Jordan had taken in over 630,000 Syrians, with the vast majority living in urban areas rather than refugee camps. Like Lebanon and Turkey, Jordan's resources were stretched thin as it provided food, shelter, and basic services to the refugees. The Zaatari refugee camp, located near the Syrian border, became one of the largest refugee camps in the world, housing over 100,000 people at its peak. Despite international aid efforts, the camp and others like it struggled to provide adequate facilities for the growing number of refugees. With limited economic resources and a strained public sector, Jordan struggled to meet the needs of both its own citizens and the growing refugee population. The refugees, many of whom were skilled workers and professionals, faced difficulties in finding employment, further adding to the economic pressures faced by local communities.

Additionally, Jordan's limited access to resources such as water has compounded the challenges posed by the refugee crisis. The country is one of the most water-scarce in the world, and the influx of refugees has further strained the country's already limited water supplies. This has made it difficult to provide basic sanitation and clean water for both refugees and host communities, contributing to the spread of diseases and creating further hardships for civilians. Jordan, a country already coping with the burden of hosting Palestinian refugees for decades, has been left in a precarious position, relying on international aid and support to manage the crisis.

Finally, Iraq has also borne the weight of the refugee crisis, though to a lesser extent than its neighbors. The ongoing instability in Iraq, compounded by its own internal conflicts and the rise of ISIS, has made it difficult for the country to absorb large numbers of Syrian refugees. However, Iraq did see an influx of Syrians seeking refuge, particularly in the Kurdish-controlled region of northern Iraq, where many Syrian Kurds fled to escape both the Assad regime and ISIS. Iraq's challenges in hosting refugees have been similar to those of Lebanon and Jordan, with strain on infrastructure, healthcare, and public services.

In conclusion, the Syrian refugee crisis has had a massive and far-reaching impact on Syria's neighboring countries. Turkey, Lebanon,

Jordan, and Iraq have all struggled to provide the necessary resources and support to the millions of displaced Syrians, while facing their own economic, political, and social challenges. The massive influx of refugees has strained public services, exacerbated sectarian and political tensions, and put enormous pressure on already fragile economies. While international aid has provided some relief, it is clear that the refugee crisis requires long-term solutions, including political resolutions to the Syrian conflict, to alleviate the strain on these countries and improve the lives of those displaced by the war.

Chapter 5
The War Within

As the Syrian civil war deepened, the internal divisions within the opposition grew increasingly pronounced, transforming the conflict from a united struggle for democratic reform into a fragmented and multifaceted war. Initially, the goal of the Syrian opposition was clear: overthrow the Assad regime and establish a more democratic and inclusive government. However, as the war dragged on, ideological, sectarian, and strategic differences began to surface, causing the opposition to splinter into multiple factions. These rifts not only weakened the overall resistance but also led to fierce infighting among various rebel groups, further complicating the path to peace. What was once a rebellion against a common enemy became a chaotic and divided battlefield where the rebels themselves became as much of an adversary as the regime.

The early days of the revolt saw the formation of broad, loosely organized coalitions, with secular and moderate groups fighting alongside Islamist factions. However, the lack of a unified command structure and the absence of a clear, overarching political agenda soon led to internal conflicts. The Free Syrian Army (FSA), initially considered the main opposition force, struggled to maintain unity as local militias and various groups with competing ideologies grew in strength. In particular, the rise of Islamist groups, such as Jabhat al-Nusra (al-Qaeda's Syrian branch) and Ahrar al-Sham, added a new and dangerous dimension to the war. While these groups shared the same ultimate goal of removing Assad, their vision for Syria's future differed drastically from the more secular or moderate factions, often advocating for an Islamic state governed by strict interpretations of Sharia law.

As the war intensified and the Assad regime continued its brutal crackdown, foreign involvement further exacerbated the internal divisions. Countries like Saudi Arabia, Qatar, and Turkey provided varying levels of support to different rebel factions, each backing groups that aligned with their own geopolitical and sectarian interests. This external support played a pivotal role in fueling the infighting, as rebel factions, rather than uniting against Assad, became increasingly loyal to their foreign backers. The competition for resources, funding, and military support created an environment where rebel groups often clashed over territory, control, and influence, further complicating the opposition's ability to mount a coherent challenge to the regime. As a result, the Syrian civil war evolved into not just a fight against the Assad regime but a war of competing ideologies and agendas, with each faction fighting not only for control of Syria but also for their vision of what that future should look like.

Factions and Fragmentation

As the Syrian civil war dragged on, the opposition to Bashar al-Assad's regime became increasingly fragmented. Initially, Syrians united under a common banner to demand political reform and the removal of the Assad family from power. However, the prolonged conflict, marked by heavy military repression, shifting allegiances, and foreign interventions, led to the fragmentation of the opposition into a wide range of factions with varying ideologies, goals, and allegiances. The failure to establish a unified opposition front created a power vacuum that made the war even more complicated, with multiple groups fighting each other in addition to the regime. This internal fragmentation not only weakened the opposition but also allowed the Assad regime to maintain its hold on power for much longer than it otherwise might have.

The Free Syrian Army (FSA), which initially represented the most prominent force of resistance against the Assad regime, soon found itself unable to effectively coordinate with the growing number of militias that began to appear on the battlefield. The FSA, a loose coalition of defected soldiers, civilian volunteers, and local militias, lacked a cohesive command structure and a clear political strategy, which made it susceptible to division. As the war continued, many local groups broke away from the FSA, leading to an increasing number of factions, each operating independently in different regions of Syria. The FSA's failure to consolidate power or establish a unified military strategy led to its gradual decline as the dominant force in the rebellion, with other, more radical factions gaining prominence.

One of the most significant causes of the fragmentation was the rise of Islamist groups. As the Assad regime intensified its brutal crackdown, the Syrian opposition began to attract fighters from various jihadist and Islamist organizations, many of whom had long opposed secularism and democracy. Among these groups, Jabhat al-Nusra (al-Qaeda's Syrian branch), and Ahrar al-Sham became two of the most influential. While they shared the ultimate goal of removing Assad, their ideological orientation differed drastically from that of the FSA and other secular factions. These Islamist factions pushed for the establishment of an Islamic state governed by their interpretation of Sharia law, a vision that put them at odds with more secular and moderate rebel groups.

The presence of these extremist groups added further complexity to the conflict. While their military effectiveness against Assad's forces was undeniable, their strict religious doctrines and brutal tactics alienated large portions of the population. The rise of ISIS (Islamic State of Iraq and Syria) further exacerbated the situation. Originally an offshoot of al-Qaeda, ISIS used the chaos of the Syrian conflict to seize large areas of land in both Syria and Iraq, declaring the establishment of a self-proclaimed caliphate in 2014. ISIS's methods were characterized by extreme violence, including mass executions, beheadings, and the subjugation of religious minorities. While their military power was significant, their authoritarian rule, which forced residents to adhere to their rigid interpretation of Islam, led to widespread resentment from both Syrians and international observers. The group's brutal tactics and desire for territorial expansion created another layer of division within the opposition, as many moderate rebels found themselves battling not only the Assad regime but also ISIS forces.

The increasing fragmentation also had a sectarian component, as different ethnic and religious groups began to assert control over regions of Syria. The Kurdish YPG (People's Defense Units), supported by the Syrian Democratic Forces (SDF), which included Kurdish, Arab, and Assyrian fighters, became a dominant force in northern Syria, particularly after the rise of ISIS. The Kurds, long marginalized by both the Assad regime and neighboring countries like Turkey, began to carve out an autonomous region known as Rojava in the northeast. The YPG's success in fighting ISIS and securing territories led to tensions with Turkey, which viewed the Kurdish groups as a threat due to their connection to the PKK (Kurdistan Workers' Party), a Kurdish separatist group. The Kurdish forces also found themselves at odds with other rebel factions that sought to maintain a unified Syrian state and resented Kurdish autonomy. The presence of Kurdish militias in the northern regions added another layer of complexity to the already fragmented landscape of Syrian opposition forces.

The international dimension of the conflict further deepened the fragmentation. As various foreign powers—including the United States, Russia, Turkey, Iran, Saudi Arabia, and Qatar—backed different rebel factions based on their strategic interests, the war became a proxy struggle, with each external power supporting specific groups that aligned with their own geopolitical goals. The U.S., for example, provided support to the Syrian Democratic Forces (SDF), primarily composed of Kurdish fighters, to fight ISIS, while Turkey supported groups aligned with the Syrian opposition but opposed Kurdish autonomy. Meanwhile, Iran's support for the Assad regime, including the deployment of Shia militia forces from Iraq, Afghanistan, and Lebanon, bolstered the regime's military capabilities, leading to a complex web of competing interests within the opposition forces themselves.

Ultimately, the fragmentation of the opposition weakened their ability to present a united front against the Assad regime, prolonging the conflict and complicating efforts to negotiate peace. This fragmentation not only hindered military effectiveness but also exacerbated the humanitarian crisis, as multiple groups fought for control of key regions, often putting civilians in harm's way. With the various factions unable or unwilling to cooperate, the conflict continued to spiral into an even more chaotic and violent struggle, leaving Syria deeply fractured and divided, with little hope for a cohesive resolution.

In conclusion, the factionalism and fragmentation within the Syrian opposition turned what began as a unified revolt against a tyrannical regime into a prolonged and multifaceted civil war. The failure to establish a unified strategy and the rise of competing ideologies and foreign interventions fragmented the opposition forces, ultimately benefiting the Assad regime, which capitalized on the infighting. The Syrian conflict became more than a struggle for power; it was a battle between competing visions of Syria's future, each faction vying for dominance in a war that devastated the country and its people.

The Rise of Extremist Groups

As the Syrian civil war unfolded, the chaos of the conflict provided fertile ground for the rise of extremist groups, which quickly filled the power vacuum left by the weakening of the central government and the fragmentation of the opposition. While the initial uprising was driven by a desire for democratic reform and political change, the escalating violence, lack of coordination within the opposition, and growing foreign interventions created a complex environment in which extremist ideologies could take root. These groups not only posed a significant threat to the stability of Syria but also to the broader Middle East, as their brutal tactics and radical agendas transformed the Syrian conflict into a global struggle against jihadist terrorism.

The first significant Islamist group to rise within the ranks of the opposition was Jabhat al-Nusra (al-Qaeda's Syrian affiliate), which emerged in 2012. Initially operating as a branch of al-Qaeda in Iraq, Jabhat al-Nusra quickly established itself as one of the most powerful and effective factions fighting the Assad regime. The group's success in recruiting both foreign fighters and local Syrians was largely due to its ability to gain the trust of local populations by providing food, medicine, and basic services in areas it controlled. While it initially presented itself as a military force fighting for the removal of Assad, Jabhat al-Nusra also sought to impose its interpretation of Islamic law in the territories it controlled, earning it both support and fear from civilians. The group's brutal tactics—such as executing prisoners, engaging in suicide bombings, and persecuting religious minorities—alienated many Syrians but also earned it significant influence, particularly in the opposition-controlled areas.

The rise of ISIS (Islamic State of Iraq and Syria) marked a major turning point in the Syrian conflict, drastically shifting the balance of power. Originally an offshoot of al-Qaeda, ISIS exploited the power vacuum left by the civil war to rapidly gain control of large areas of Syria and Iraq, declaring the establishment of a self-proclaimed caliphate in 2014. ISIS's ideology was built on a strict, literal interpretation of Islam, and its goal was to establish a global Islamic state governed by its interpretation of Sharia law. Unlike other rebel factions, which were primarily focused on removing Assad, ISIS was more interested in controlling territory, implementing its version of an Islamic state, and challenging the broader regional and global order.

The rise of ISIS had a profound impact on the dynamics of the conflict. The group's military success, coupled with its brutal tactics, including mass executions, beheadings, and the enslavement of women and children, made it one of the most feared and notorious groups in the world. It also attracted thousands of foreign fighters, many of whom were drawn to its apocalyptic vision of jihad and its ability to offer a sense of purpose in the context of the war. At its peak, ISIS controlled large swaths of northern and eastern Syria, including the city of Raqqa, which it declared as the capital of its caliphate. The group's rapid territorial expansion and its ability to govern its captured areas made it one of the most formidable forces in the conflict. However, its rise also led to widespread international intervention, with a U.S.-led coalition, alongside Kurdish and local forces, launching an all-out campaign to defeat the group.

Despite its territorial losses in recent years, ISIS's impact on the Syrian conflict remains significant. Its brutality and ability to radicalize young recruits have left a lasting legacy on both Syria and the broader Middle East. The group's presence exacerbated sectarian divisions in Syria, as it targeted religious and ethnic minorities, including Christians, Yazidis, and Shia Muslims, for persecution, forced conversion, and execution. ISIS also contributed to the militarization of the Syrian conflict, as many opposition groups were forced to fight not only against the Assad regime but also against the growing threat of ISIS's expanding territorial control.

In addition to Jabhat al-Nusra and ISIS, other extremist factions have emerged throughout the course of the war, further complicating the conflict. Groups such as Hayat Tahrir al-Sham (HTS), a successor to Jabhat al-Nusra, have continued to fight for control of regions in Syria's northwest, particularly in Idlib, which became one of the last major opposition strongholds. HTS, which maintains ties to al-Qaeda, has been involved in both fighting the Assad regime and clashing with other rebel factions in the area. The presence of such groups has further fragmented the opposition, with moderate factions often caught in the middle of battles between extremists and the regime's forces. The rise of these extremist groups has also drawn the attention of regional powers, including Turkey, Iran, and Russia, all of whom have sought to exert influence over these groups for their own strategic purposes.

The presence of extremist groups has made the conflict in Syria even more intractable and deadly. These groups, while initially successful in their military campaigns, have contributed to the brutalization of Syrian society. Their presence has complicated international efforts to broker a political solution to the war, as many countries—particularly the U.S., Russia, and regional actors—have struggled to navigate their support for various factions in the conflict. The fight against extremism has become a key part of the international response to the war, with efforts to defeat ISIS and similar groups drawing in military interventions from global powers, but without addressing the underlying causes of the conflict, such as political repression and sectarianism, which have allowed such groups to thrive.

In conclusion, the rise of extremist groups in Syria has profoundly reshaped the conflict, turning it into not only a battle for the future of Syria but also a global struggle against jihadist terrorism. Groups like Jabhat al-Nusra and ISIS have exploited the chaos of the war to seize territory, recruit fighters, and impose their radical ideologies, while also deepening sectarian divisions and complicating efforts to find a political solution to the conflict. The impact of these extremist groups extends far beyond Syria's borders, as their actions have destabilized the region and posed a significant threat to international security.

Power Struggles Among the Rebels

As the Syrian civil war progressed, the lack of unity within the opposition forces became a significant obstacle to their efforts to overthrow the Assad regime. While initially united by a shared desire for political reform and an end to authoritarian rule, the Syrian rebels soon found themselves divided along ideological, sectarian, and strategic lines. The complex power struggles among the various rebel factions not only weakened the opposition but also prolonged the war, making it easier for the Assad regime to maintain its grip on power. As different groups jostled for influence, control over territory, and foreign backing, the unity of purpose that initially united them was lost, and the Syrian rebels became as fragmented and divided as the nation they sought to liberate.

One of the main reasons for the internal divisions within the rebel forces was the ideological diversity among the factions. Initially, the opposition included a mix of secular groups, moderate Islamists, and hardline jihadists, each with different visions for Syria's future. The Free Syrian Army (FSA), which was one of the earliest and largest groups to take up arms against Assad, was initially a broad coalition of defected soldiers and civilian volunteers. Its primary goal was the removal of Assad and the establishment of a democratic, secular Syria. However, the FSA struggled with internal cohesion due to its lack of a clear command structure and the absence of a unified political agenda. As the war dragged on, the FSA's influence waned as more radical and organized factions, particularly Islamist groups, began to rise in prominence.

Islamist groups, such as Jabhat al-Nusra (al-Qaeda's Syrian affiliate), Ahrar al-Sham, and later ISIS, introduced an entirely different agenda, advocating for the establishment of an Islamic state governed by strict interpretations of Sharia law. These groups viewed the secular and moderate opposition factions as insufficiently committed to their vision of a religiously based society. This led to ideological clashes, with some Islamist groups seeking to eliminate more moderate factions that they viewed as apostates. This created a toxic environment of mistrust and competition, as many rebel groups found themselves battling not just Assad's forces but also each other.

The lack of centralized leadership and coordination within the opposition also fueled power struggles among the rebels. The formation of local militias and smaller groups allowed for more flexibility and regional autonomy but also meant that these factions operated independently, often without coordination or common objectives. Local commanders were able to exercise significant influence over the militias they led, which further fragmented the overall opposition. As a result, these groups frequently fought over territory, resources, and access to foreign aid. In areas where multiple factions operated, competition for dominance often led to violent clashes between rebels, weakening their overall military capability and preventing them from effectively challenging the Assad regime.

In addition to ideological and strategic divides, foreign influence played a major role in the internal power struggles among the rebel factions. International actors, including Saudi Arabia, Qatar, Turkey, and the United States, became involved in the conflict, providing varying degrees of military, financial, and logistical support to different factions. These foreign backers often chose sides based on their own geopolitical interests, further exacerbating divisions within the opposition. Saudi Arabia and Qatar, for instance, provided significant support to Islamist groups, while the U.S. and its allies tended to back more moderate factions, though this support was often inconsistent and fragmented. The rivalry between regional powers and their competing interests in Syria created an environment where rebel groups were not only fighting Assad's forces but also each other for the favor of foreign backers. This external involvement fueled internal factionalism, with some rebel groups becoming more beholden to their foreign patrons than to the broader cause of removing Assad.

The lack of a unified command structure and coherent political vision also hindered the ability of the opposition to establish an effective governance system in the areas they controlled. While some rebel factions were able to administer local services, others were more focused on military victories than on the needs of the population. This inconsistency in governance and the failure to provide basic services further alienated civilians in opposition-held areas. The inability of the opposition to present a united front not only limited their military effectiveness but also prevented them from building trust with the civilian population, who were often caught in the crossfire between competing rebel factions.

The power struggles among the rebel groups also contributed to the rise of extremist factions. As more moderate groups were weakened or sidelined by internal infighting, extremist groups like ISIS and Jabhat al-Nusra found an opening to expand their influence. These groups offered an alternative vision of governance, often promising a more organized and coherent rule under their interpretation of Islamic law. Their ability to project military strength, alongside their use of brutal tactics to suppress rivals, enabled them to gain control over large swaths of territory. However, the rise of ISIS, in particular, further exacerbated the divisions within the opposition, as many rebel groups found themselves forced to confront not just Assad but also the growing threat of jihadist extremism within their own ranks.

In conclusion, the power struggles among Syria's rebel factions played a central role in the prolongation of the war and the fragmentation of the opposition. The ideological divides, lack of centralized leadership, and foreign interventions created a deeply divided opposition, where factions fought as much against each other as they did against the Assad regime. The infighting, combined with the rise of extremist groups, undermined the ability of the opposition to mount a coherent challenge to the regime, and in many cases, it allowed the Assad government to maintain control over much of Syria. These internal divisions continue to have lasting effects on the Syrian conflict, making a political resolution increasingly difficult to achieve.

Chapter 6
The Role of International Powers

The Syrian civil war, initially a domestic uprising against a brutal regime, quickly evolved into a global conflict, drawing in international powers with competing interests and goals. From the early days of the conflict, foreign actors saw the war in Syria not only as a humanitarian crisis but also as a geopolitical battleground. As various countries provided military, financial, and diplomatic support to either the Assad regime or opposition factions, Syria became a proxy war for broader regional and global struggles. The involvement of international powers complicated an already complex civil war, deepening the divisions within Syria and delaying any chance for a peaceful resolution.

At the heart of the international struggle stood Russia and Iran, two of the most steadfast allies of the Assad regime. Russia, with its long-standing strategic interests in the region, sought to maintain its military and diplomatic influence in Syria, where it has a naval base in Tartus, and to counter U.S. influence in the Middle East. Russia's intervention in 2015 marked a turning point in the conflict. By providing air support, weapons, and diplomatic cover at the United Nations Security Council, Russia ensured the survival of the Assad regime despite significant battlefield losses. Iran, similarly, offered crucial backing through financial aid, weapons, and the deployment of military personnel and proxy forces such as Hezbollah. For both

Russia and Iran, Syria was not only a battlefield but also a key pillar in their broader strategy to shape the Middle East according to their interests, particularly in countering the influence of the U.S. and Sunni Arab powers.

On the other side of the conflict, Western and regional powers, including the United States, Turkey, Saudi Arabia, and Qatar, supported various opposition factions, each with their own set of objectives. The U.S., initially hesitant to intervene directly, began providing aid to moderate rebel groups and later focused its efforts on defeating ISIS. The U.S. led a coalition of international forces that supported the Syrian Democratic Forces (SDF), primarily composed of Kurdish fighters, to combat ISIS's territorial expansion. Meanwhile, Turkey sought to limit Kurdish autonomy in Syria and focused on supporting Sunni rebel factions to challenge Assad, viewing the Syrian Kurdish forces as a threat to its own territorial integrity. Saudi Arabia and Qatar funneled resources to Islamist groups, with the goal of weakening Iran's influence in Syria and countering Assad's Shia-aligned government. These foreign interventions, while intended to counterbalance each other, also created a situation where Syria's future was largely being shaped by external powers, each pursuing its own interests without a coherent strategy for peace.

The involvement of international powers in the Syrian conflict transformed it from a domestic struggle into a global struggle for influence. While foreign support helped to sustain different factions in the war, it also complicated the conflict, with shifting alliances, changing priorities, and competing agendas. The result was a war that could not be resolved on Syrian terms alone. The international powers' vested interests in Syria's future continue to shape the war's trajectory, making any prospect of peace increasingly difficult to achieve.

Russia's Support for Assad

Russia's support for the Assad regime in Syria has been one of the most decisive factors in the prolonged nature of the Syrian conflict. From the early days of the civil war, Russia saw its relationship with Syria not just in terms of geopolitical alliances but also through the lens of its broader strategic interests in the Middle East. As a key ally of President Bashar al-Assad's regime, Russia's military, financial, and diplomatic backing helped keep the regime in power despite substantial territorial losses to the opposition and the rise of extremist groups like ISIS. Russia's support for Assad was rooted in a complex mix of regional influence, the protection of military assets, and an ideological commitment to preserving the sovereignty of states, even when those states are authoritarian regimes.

Russia's involvement in Syria long predates the civil war, with Syria serving as one of Russia's few remaining allies in the Middle East. Since the Soviet era, Syria has been a cornerstone of Russia's influence in the region, offering a naval base in Tartus and a foothold in the Arab world. This long-standing relationship made Syria crucial to Russia's strategic objectives, particularly its efforts to maintain its influence in the Mediterranean and balance against Western influence in the region. When the uprising against Assad's rule began in 2011, Russia saw the potential collapse of the Assad regime as a blow to its regional interests and a threat to its broader geopolitical ambitions. As such, Russia's initial response was to provide diplomatic backing for Assad in international forums, using its veto power at the United Nations Security Council (UNSC) to block resolutions aimed at condemning Assad or imposing sanctions.

The turning point in Russia's involvement came in 2015, when the Assad regime appeared on the brink of collapse. After years of battlefield losses and dwindling resources, Assad's forces were increasingly reliant on external support. At this critical juncture, Russia intervened militarily, launching airstrikes and providing logistical support to bolster Assad's position. The Russian air campaign began in September 2015, with Russian fighter jets and bombers targeting both opposition groups and extremist factions, such as ISIS, but also striking moderate and secular rebel groups, which was controversial internationally. While Russia claimed that its primary objective was to fight ISIS, many of its airstrikes were directed at opposition-held areas, further bolstering the Assad regime's control.

Russia's military intervention was crucial in reversing the fortunes of the Syrian government. By deploying its advanced airpower, Russia was able to conduct airstrikes that directly impacted the battlefield, enabling Assad's forces to reclaim key cities and territories from rebel groups. Russia also provided significant military assistance in the form of weapons, training, and intelligence to Assad's forces, helping them gain the upper hand over the opposition. The Russian presence on the ground, particularly in the form of military advisors and personnel, played a pivotal role in ensuring the regime's military coherence, preventing the complete disintegration of the Syrian military structure.

Beyond direct military intervention, Russia's support for Assad was also marked by its ongoing diplomatic efforts. Russia consistently framed its involvement as a defense of Syrian sovereignty, arguing that the international community should respect Syria's right to determine its own future without foreign interference. This stance was consistent with Russia's broader foreign policy goals, which emphasize state sovereignty and non-intervention, especially when it concerns regimes that are aligned with Russian interests. In this context, Russia portrayed its actions in Syria as part of a broader ideological campaign to resist Western-led efforts to topple authoritarian regimes under the guise of promoting democracy. By consistently opposing Western-backed efforts to force Assad out of power, Russia aligned itself with the narrative that interventionism had exacerbated instability in the region, citing Libya and Iraq as examples of failed Western policies.

Russia's role in Syria was also influenced by its desire to maintain its position as a global power with a say in Middle Eastern affairs. The Syrian conflict allowed Russia to reassert itself on the global stage, challenging the influence of the United States and its allies in the region. The Kremlin capitalized on the vacuum created by Western reluctance to intervene in Syria, positioning itself as the main power broker in the Middle East. Through its military and diplomatic support for Assad, Russia strengthened its strategic partnership with Iran, which also supported the Syrian regime, and played a central role in shaping the political landscape of Syria. The Russian-led Astana talks, which brought together Iran, Turkey, and Syria to negotiate ceasefires and de-escalation zones, reflected Russia's attempt to manage the conflict and influence the outcome of the war.

While Russia's intervention helped stabilize the Assad regime, it also deepened the complexities of the Syrian war. Russian support, particularly in the form of airstrikes, not only targeted rebel forces but also resulted in substantial civilian casualties and the destruction of civilian infrastructure. Cities like Aleppo and Homs were severely damaged by Russian bombardments, exacerbating the humanitarian crisis and displacing millions of people. Russia's military actions also put it at odds with other international powers, particularly the United

States and European Union, which supported opposition groups and condemned Russia's role in the war. Furthermore, Russia's growing influence in Syria led to tensions with regional powers, such as Turkey and Israel, each of which had its own interests in the conflict.

In conclusion, Russia's support for the Assad regime has been a decisive factor in the Syrian civil war. By providing military, financial, and diplomatic backing, Russia helped to preserve Assad's rule and shift the balance of power in his favor. Russia's involvement has not only solidified its position as a key player in the Middle East but has also deepened the geopolitical divide between global powers, particularly with the United States and its allies. While Russia's intervention helped the Assad regime reclaim significant territory, it also contributed to the immense human suffering and destruction that has marked Syria's ongoing war.

The U.S. and the West: A Changing Strategy

From the outset of the Syrian civil war in 2011, the United States and Western powers initially took a passive approach, hesitant to directly intervene in the conflict. The initial strategy was to support diplomatic efforts aimed at resolving the crisis and to push for political reform through the United Nations and other international institutions. However, as the war intensified and the humanitarian crisis deepened, the West's strategy began to shift. The rise of extremist groups, particularly ISIS, and the increasing instability in the region forced the United States and its allies to reevaluate their approach to Syria, moving from cautious diplomacy to active military involvement. This shifting strategy was driven by a mix of humanitarian concerns, the fight against terrorism, and broader geopolitical interests in the Middle East.

In the early years of the conflict, the U.S. and its European allies were focused on diplomatic efforts to isolate the Assad regime and encourage its ouster. Initially, the Obama administration and European countries called for Assad to step down, viewing his brutal repression of peaceful protesters as unacceptable. However, as the opposition became more fragmented and the war turned into an all-out civil conflict, the West's approach began to evolve. While the U.S. imposed sanctions on the Syrian regime, including economic sanctions aimed at weakening Assad's hold on power, there was no direct military intervention. The Obama administration emphasized the importance of a political solution to the crisis, supporting the efforts of the United Nations to broker peace talks between the opposition and the regime. However, these diplomatic efforts largely failed to produce results, as both sides were entrenched in their positions, and Assad, with the backing of Russia and Iran, was able to hold onto power.

The turning point for U.S. strategy came with the rise of ISIS in 2014. The group's rapid territorial expansion across Syria and Iraq, its brutal tactics, and its declaration of a caliphate in the heart of the Middle East created a new set of priorities for Western powers. The U.S. quickly shifted from focusing solely on the removal of Assad to confronting the threat posed by ISIS. The Obama administration, after initial hesitations, authorized airstrikes against ISIS positions in Syria, as part of a broader campaign to weaken the group's hold on territory. In addition to airstrikes, the U.S. provided support to Syrian rebel groups, including Kurdish forces, as part of an effort to retake territory from ISIS. The creation of the Syrian Democratic Forces (SDF), an alliance of Kurdish and Arab fighters, became a focal point of U.S. military strategy in Syria, with the U.S. providing arms, training, and air support to these forces as they fought to reclaim ISIS-controlled areas.

However, the U.S. involvement in Syria became increasingly complicated as it found itself supporting a diverse set of rebel groups, some of which were in direct opposition to Assad's forces, while others, like the Kurdish YPG, were targeted by Turkey, a NATO ally. This created a complex web of alliances and rivalries, making it difficult for the U.S. to pursue a consistent and coherent strategy. While the U.S. and its allies focused on defeating ISIS, they also had to contend with the Assad regime, which was receiving support from Russia and Iran. The West's strategy became one of balancing multiple, often conflicting, goals: defeating ISIS, supporting opposition groups, and addressing the larger question of Assad's future.

By 2016, with ISIS on the verge of losing significant territory in both Syria and Iraq, the focus of U.S. policy began to shift once again. While the defeat of ISIS remained a priority, the U.S. began to increasingly acknowledge the necessity of dealing with the Assad regime and its supporters. The Trump administration, which took office in January 2017, further complicated the West's position in Syria. Despite initially signaling a more aggressive stance toward Assad, including a missile strike on a Syrian airbase in response to a chemical weapons attack in Khan Sheikhoun, the Trump administration was also focused on withdrawing U.S. forces from Syria. The decision to pull back from Syria in late 2018, which saw the U.S. abandoning Kurdish allies in the northeast to face a Turkish offensive, exemplified the shifting priorities and uncertainty in U.S. policy. The abandonment of Kurdish forces created a rift between the U.S. and its allies, as many saw it as a betrayal, while others argued that the U.S. should no longer bear the responsibility for stabilizing Syria.

Throughout the conflict, the Western strategy in Syria has been shaped by several competing factors. The fight against terrorism, particularly ISIS, has been the central objective, but efforts to end the Assad regime have been consistently undermined by both the Russian and Iranian-backed support for Assad. Moreover, the complex geopolitics of the region, with the involvement of Turkey, Iran, and Russia, has made it difficult for Western powers to formulate a unified and consistent approach. The challenge of balancing support for local partners like the Kurds with the broader geopolitical need to counter Russia and Iran has complicated U.S. policy. Furthermore, the humanitarian crisis, with millions of refugees and internally displaced persons, has forced the West to consider its role in providing aid and stabilizing the region.

In conclusion, the shifting strategy of the United States and Western powers in Syria reflects the changing nature of the conflict and the complex interplay of military, political, and humanitarian factors. What began as a focus on diplomacy and the removal of Assad transformed into a military campaign against ISIS, and later, a more nuanced engagement with Assad's regime. As the war has evolved, Western strategy has continued to shift in response to new threats, shifting alliances, and the broader geopolitical dynamics of the Middle East. The absence of a clear, consistent strategy, combined with competing priorities, has made it difficult for the West to achieve its goals in Syria, leaving the country divided and unstable with no clear path to peace.

The Proxy War: Iran and the Middle East

The Syrian civil war, which erupted in 2011, became a pivotal moment in the broader Middle Eastern geopolitical struggle, especially as Iran significantly increased its involvement in the conflict. As one of Bashar al-Assad's most steadfast allies, Iran's role in Syria is a key element of its broader strategy to influence the region. Iran's support for the Assad regime turned Syria into a battleground for a larger proxy war, where regional and global powers aligned themselves with different factions to advance their own interests. For Iran, maintaining Assad's regime was a critical component of its broader ambition to expand its influence across the Middle East, consolidate Shia power, and counter the influence of Sunni powers like Saudi Arabia and Western-backed states. This proxy war has had profound implications not only for Syria but also for the region as a whole.

Iran's involvement in Syria began in earnest as soon as the conflict broke out. As a close ally of the Assad family, Iran viewed the uprising against the regime as a threat to its interests in the region. Syria has long been a crucial ally for Iran, providing a land bridge to the Lebanese group Hezbollah, which Iran has supported for decades. Hezbollah is seen by Iran as a key player in its efforts to influence Lebanon and maintain a resistance front against Israel. Therefore, maintaining a friendly government in Damascus was vital to Iran's broader regional strategy. Tehran's support for the Assad regime was motivated by its desire to preserve this vital corridor, while also solidifying its influence over the Levant, especially in the face of growing Sunni Arab powers like Saudi Arabia and Qatar, which were backing the opposition.

Iran's support for Assad extended beyond mere diplomatic backing; it included substantial military and financial aid. Iran provided the regime with crucial logistical support, weapons, and personnel to help combat the opposition. Tehran deployed Qods Force, an elite unit of the Islamic Revolutionary Guard Corps (IRGC), to provide direct military assistance. This included training, intelligence, and tactical support to the Syrian military and pro-regime militias. Iran also coordinated the deployment of Hezbollah fighters from Lebanon, bolstering Assad's forces in critical battles, particularly in areas like Homs and Aleppo. Over time, Iran also facilitated the recruitment and deployment of Shia militias from Iraq, Afghanistan, and Pakistan, further reinforcing Assad's forces. These efforts allowed the Syrian government to withstand significant pressure from opposition forces and extremist groups like ISIS, helping to tip the balance of the war in Assad's favor.

Iran's involvement in the Syrian conflict is also part of a broader regional strategy to extend its influence over the Middle East. The so-called "Shia Crescent," a term often used by Iranian officials, refers to a belt of Shia-majority or Shia-dominated areas that stretches from Iran through Iraq, Syria, and Lebanon. Iran sees the defense of the Assad regime as crucial to the survival of this Shia-dominated alliance, as it provides Tehran with direct access to Hezbollah in Lebanon and ensures a Shia-controlled corridor running from Iran's borders to the Mediterranean. This strategic corridor not only enhances Iran's regional power but also positions Iran as a leading actor in the Middle East, capable of countering the influence of Sunni-majority countries, such as Saudi Arabia, and Western powers.

The Iranian intervention in Syria has had wide-reaching consequences for the region. One of the most significant effects has been the intensification of the sectarian divide in the Middle East. The war in Syria is not just a civil war but also a reflection of the larger Sunni-Shia divide, which has been a defining feature of Middle Eastern geopolitics for centuries. Iran's support for the Shia-led Assad regime and the involvement of Shia militias in Syria further exacerbated sectarian tensions across the region. Sunni-majority countries, particularly Saudi Arabia, viewed Iran's actions in Syria as an attempt to assert Shia dominance and increase Iranian influence in the Arab world. This led to heightened tensions between Iran and Saudi Arabia, which had been locked in a broader regional power struggle long before the war in Syria began.

Furthermore, Iran's involvement in Syria has directly influenced the dynamics of the regional conflict in Iraq, Lebanon, and Yemen. In Iraq, Iran has backed Shia militias in the fight against ISIS, cementing its influence in the country following the fall of Saddam Hussein. In Lebanon, Iran's support for Hezbollah has allowed the group to grow stronger, solidifying its position as a powerful political and military force in the region. In Yemen, Iran's support for the Houthi rebels has been seen as part of its strategy to counter Saudi influence, further embedding itself in the region's sectarian struggles. Iran's involvement in these various theaters has resulted in a significant increase in its regional footprint, positioning it as the preeminent power in the Middle East, particularly among Shia-dominated states and groups.

In conclusion, Iran's support for the Assad regime in Syria has been a key factor in the prolongation of the civil war and the transformation of the conflict into a broader regional proxy war. Iran's military, financial, and logistical support for Assad has helped stabilize the regime and secure Iran's strategic interests in the region, particularly its access to Hezbollah and its role in the Shia Crescent. However, this involvement has also contributed to the deepening of sectarian divides and the ongoing geopolitical struggle between Iran and Sunni Arab powers, particularly Saudi Arabia. The Syrian conflict has become a proxy battleground for larger regional and global struggles, and Iran's role in the war continues to shape the future of the Middle East.

Chapter 7
The Collapse of the State

The Syrian civil war, which began in 2011 as an uprising against the authoritarian regime of Bashar al-Assad, gradually transformed into a full-blown civil conflict, and by the mid-2010s, it had become a war of survival for both the state and its people. The prolonged violence, internal divisions, and foreign interventions weakened Syria's institutional structure, leading to the collapse of the state in many parts of the country. The once-powerful central government, which had maintained control over much of Syria for decades, began to lose its grip on power as the war escalated, fragmented, and regionalized. The collapse of the Syrian state marked the end of Assad's ability to govern effectively, and with it came the breakdown of law, order, and basic services for millions of Syrians.

As the fighting intensified, large swaths of Syria fell under the control of opposition groups, extremist factions like ISIS, and Kurdish forces. In many areas, the government's authority became increasingly symbolic, and local militias or armed groups took over administrative functions. In opposition-held regions, governance was often carried out by local councils or foreign-backed rebel factions, while extremist groups like ISIS implemented their own brutal, authoritarian rule, imposing a strict version of Sharia law. Meanwhile, in Kurdish-controlled areas, the Syrian Democratic Forces (SDF) established their own governance structures, which at times conflicted with both Assad's regime and other opposition factions. This fragmentation of power contributed significantly to the collapse of central governance, leaving the country divided and unstable.

The collapse of the state was not only political but also economic and social. The Syrian economy, once relatively stable and diversified, was decimated by years of war. The regime's reliance on heavy-handed military tactics and the destruction of critical infrastructure caused widespread unemployment, hyperinflation, and a collapse in essential services. Cities like Aleppo and Homs, once thriving centers of commerce and industry, were reduced to rubble. The breakdown of healthcare, education, and utilities left millions of Syrians living in dire conditions, with little access to basic needs. The failure of the central government to provide security and services exacerbated the suffering of civilians, leading to mass displacement and a refugee crisis that spilled over into neighboring countries and beyond. The collapse of the state in Syria created a power vacuum, and the country became an ungovernable, fractured space where survival was the primary concern for most of its people.

The Breakdown of Infrastructure

The Syrian civil war has had a devastating impact on the country's infrastructure, with widespread destruction and collapse affecting virtually every aspect of daily life. What was once a modern state with cities like Aleppo and Damascus serving as regional hubs of commerce and culture has been transformed into a war-torn landscape, where basic services and infrastructure no longer function effectively. From airstrikes and artillery bombardments to sieges and ground offensives, the destruction of infrastructure has been one of the most tangible consequences of the conflict. The collapse of infrastructure not only undermined the Syrian government's ability to control the country but also worsened the humanitarian crisis, leaving millions of civilians without access to essential services and exacerbating the suffering of an already devastated population.

One of the most visible and critical forms of infrastructure destruction has been the damage to housing and residential areas. Cities like Aleppo, Homs, and Idlib, once vibrant urban centers, have been heavily bombarded and reduced to rubble. Government airstrikes, artillery shelling, and aerial bombings aimed at opposition-held areas have left entire neighborhoods uninhabitable. Residential buildings, schools, hospitals, and markets have been destroyed, forcing civilians to flee and leading to the mass displacement of populations. By 2016, over 50 percent of Syria's housing stock had been destroyed or damaged, and the lack of shelter for millions of displaced persons worsened the refugee crisis, both inside Syria and in neighboring countries. Many Syrians were forced to live in makeshift shelters, including tents, abandoned buildings, or even in overcrowded refugee camps where conditions were dire.

Another significant area of infrastructure breakdown was energy production and distribution. Before the conflict, Syria had a relatively stable energy grid, with oil, natural gas, and electricity powering homes, businesses, and industries. However, the war has severely damaged the country's energy infrastructure, including oil refineries, power plants, and pipelines. The Syrian government's reliance on military control of energy sources led to attacks on key infrastructure by both rebel and government forces. Areas under opposition control often found their access to electricity and fuel cut off, while government-held territories faced shortages due to damage to production facilities. The rise of ISIS further compounded this issue, as the group seized control of major oil fields in eastern Syria, depriving the government of critical revenue and leaving many Syrians without access to basic energy resources. As of 2020, Syria's energy sector was operating at a fraction of its pre-war capacity, with widespread power outages becoming a daily reality for most Syrians.

The destruction of healthcare facilities has also had a devastating impact on Syria's infrastructure. Prior to the war, Syria had a relatively advanced healthcare system, with numerous hospitals and medical centers spread across the country. However, since the conflict began, healthcare facilities have been systematically targeted, both by the Syrian government and opposition groups. Airstrikes have destroyed hospitals, clinics, and medical supplies, leaving health workers and civilians vulnerable to injury and disease. The World Health Organization (WHO) reported that by 2016, at least 400 healthcare facilities had been damaged or destroyed. The destruction of healthcare infrastructure, coupled with a severe shortage of medical professionals and supplies, has led to a healthcare crisis, with many Syrians unable to access life-saving treatment. Hospitals that remain operational often face overcrowded conditions, lack of essential medicines, and insufficient staff. The collapse of the healthcare system has meant that basic services, such as maternal care, vaccinations, and treatment for chronic illnesses, have become scarce.

The war has also led to the breakdown of education infrastructure. Schools have been destroyed by bombings or used as shelters for displaced populations, leaving millions of Syrian children without access to education. The United Nations Children's Fund (UNICEF) reported that over 2 million children were out of school by 2016, a staggering figure that continues to rise as the war persists. Education facilities have become targets for both government and opposition forces, with the bombing of schools being used as a tactic of intimidation and control. As a result, a generation of Syrians has missed out on education, contributing to the long-term challenges of rebuilding the country's future. Many children have been forced into labor or have become soldiers for rebel or extremist groups. The destruction of schools has also had a broader social impact, as education is vital for rebuilding society and developing a workforce that can help in the post-conflict reconstruction of Syria.

Finally, water and sanitation systems have also been severely damaged. In the early stages of the war, the Syrian government's military operations targeted water treatment plants and distribution networks to undermine the opposition's access to basic resources. Rebels, in turn, cut off access to water in government-controlled areas. The result was widespread shortages, contamination, and inadequate sanitation. The loss of access to clean water has led to outbreaks of waterborne diseases, including cholera and typhoid, particularly in areas where civilians are trapped by fighting or living in refugee camps. With no functioning water treatment systems and widespread infrastructure damage, access to clean drinking water has become a luxury for many Syrians.

In conclusion, the breakdown of infrastructure in Syria has been one of the most catastrophic aspects of the ongoing civil war. The destruction of homes, energy facilities, hospitals, schools, and water systems has crippled the country, worsening the already dire humanitarian crisis. The collapse of infrastructure has not only made life unbearable for millions of Syrians but also created significant barriers to any potential recovery. Rebuilding Syria's infrastructure will require immense international support, investment, and cooperation, as well as a long-term commitment to ensuring that future generations of Syrians have access to the resources and services necessary for a stable and prosperous society.

The Disintegration of Government Control

As the Syrian civil war evolved from peaceful protests to a full-scale military conflict, the Assad regime's once-strong grip on power began to erode. The disintegration of government control, both in terms of territorial sovereignty and political authority, became one of the most significant outcomes of the war. Initially, the government was able to maintain control over major cities like Damascus and Aleppo, as well as the central and coastal regions of Syria. However, as the conflict dragged on, and as various factions emerged to challenge Assad's rule, the regime's control steadily weakened. This breakdown in control not only fractured the country but also led to a growing sense of lawlessness, chaos, and fragmentation.

At the start of the uprising, the Syrian government was strong, with a centralized military and intelligence apparatus capable of suppressing any form of dissent. However, as protests spread and opposition groups began to form in the wake of the regime's violent crackdown, the government's capacity to maintain control over the entire country began to falter. The Free Syrian Army (FSA), initially composed of defected soldiers and civilian volunteers, began to launch attacks on government forces, targeting military checkpoints and other symbols of Assad's authority. As the conflict escalated and foreign-backed opposition forces grew in number and strength, the government's military strength was stretched thin across multiple fronts. The regime began losing control of various cities and towns, particularly in the rural areas, where local militias and rebel factions took over. These areas, once under the control of the central government, soon became no-go zones for the regime, and government forces were unable to mount effective counterattacks.

By 2013, regional fragmentation became one of the most pronounced features of the war, with different parts of the country falling into the hands of various rebel groups, foreign powers, and local militias. Large sections of northern and eastern Syria came under the control of ISIS and Jabhat al-Nusra (al-Qaeda's affiliate in Syria), while the Syrian Democratic Forces (SDF), primarily Kurdish-led, took control of key areas in the north. These groups not only challenged the Syrian government militarily but also established their own governance structures in the territories they controlled. As the government lost control over more territory, it became increasingly reliant on its military and security services to maintain order in the areas it still controlled, such as Damascus, Homs, and along the coastal areas. The growing inability of the regime to administer and govern the vast parts of the country that it had lost further highlighted the disintegration of its control.

The loss of key infrastructure was also a critical factor in the disintegration of government control. As rebel groups and extremist factions seized towns and villages, they often took control of important infrastructure such as hospitals, schools, energy plants, and communication networks. In many cases, these areas were isolated from the central government, and local militias or opposition groups took over the administration of services. The government struggled to maintain access to these regions, as opposition forces frequently destroyed or sabotaged critical infrastructure to prevent the government from re-establishing control. This not only disrupted the daily lives of civilians but also made it increasingly difficult for the government to project power and influence over the entire country.

One of the most significant contributors to the collapse of government control was foreign intervention. While the regime had support from Iran and Hezbollah, which provided military and financial assistance, it also faced opposition from an array of foreign-backed groups. The United States, Saudi Arabia, Qatar, and Turkey provided varying levels of support to the opposition, further weakening the central government's hold over territory. This support, particularly from Western countries and regional Sunni powers, created a direct challenge to the Assad regime, as they actively backed rebel forces seeking to overthrow him. Meanwhile, Russia's intervention in 2015 played a decisive role in propping up the Assad regime militarily, providing airstrikes, weapons, and logistical support. However, the presence of multiple foreign powers supporting opposing factions made it increasingly difficult for the Syrian government to consolidate its control, as different regions became battlefields for competing interests.

The disintegration of government authority also manifested in the breakdown of the rule of law. In areas controlled by rebel factions, governance structures began to emerge, often based on local councils or military command. While these councils and militias often provided basic services and attempted to establish their own order, the lack of central authority meant that lawlessness, corruption, and human rights violations were rampant. In many cases, opposition groups resorted to harsh methods of control, such as executions, torture, and the suppression of dissent. Similarly, in areas controlled by ISIS, the imposition of strict Sharia law and the use of violence to enforce obedience meant that the traditional rule of law had been entirely supplanted by extremist interpretations of governance. The collapse of the state's authority was not just a loss of military control; it also meant that Syrians were forced to live under the often brutal and chaotic rule of warlords, militias, and extremist factions.

Finally, the collapse of governance and security also led to widespread displacement. As the government lost control over key regions, millions of Syrians were forced to flee their homes in search of safety. The inability of the regime to maintain control over the countryside, combined with the targeting of civilian populations by both government and rebel forces, led to the mass exodus of Syrians. This displacement, both within Syria and to neighboring countries, created a refugee crisis of monumental proportions, further undermining the ability of the government to maintain any semblance of control.

In conclusion, the disintegration of government control in Syria has been a critical factor in the country's descent into chaos. The regime's inability to retain control over vast portions of territory, the loss of infrastructure, and the influence of foreign actors all contributed to the erosion of Assad's power. This fragmentation has not only prolonged the war but has also created a fractured and deeply unstable environment, where lawlessness, sectarian violence, and extreme ideologies have flourished. The collapse of Syria's state institutions has created a power vacuum that continues to impact the country's ability to rebuild and recover, even as the conflict moves toward its tenth year.

Lawlessness and the Rise of Militias

As the Syrian civil war raged on, the collapse of state authority and the breakdown of the rule of law created a fertile environment for the rise of militias. With the Assad regime's military forces stretched thin and unable to maintain control over much of the country, local militias began to fill the vacuum left by the central government. These militias, made up of both opposition fighters and pro-regime loyalists, often took control of towns, villages, and neighborhoods, operating with little regard for central authority or established laws. What began as small, localized defense groups soon grew into powerful, armed factions that often governed through violence and intimidation, further contributing to Syria's lawlessness and instability.

In opposition-controlled areas, the rise of militias was driven by the need to protect local populations from both the regime's forces and extremist factions. Early on, these militias were formed from defectors of the Syrian Army, civilian volunteers, and tribal groups, united by a common goal to overthrow Bashar al-Assad and his regime. As the war progressed, these groups became more organized, though they remained largely autonomous. Many of these militias lacked centralized command structures, and as a result, they were often motivated by local interests, political ideologies, or sectarian affiliations. The Free Syrian Army (FSA) was one of the first major armed opposition groups, but it quickly splintered as different factions emerged with varying degrees of radicalization. Some groups, such as Ahrar al-Sham and Jabhat al-Nusra, began to impose more rigid interpretations of Islamic law and adopted more extreme tactics, further fracturing the opposition and exacerbating the lawlessness.

The rise of Islamic State (ISIS) in Syria also played a significant role in this dynamic. As ISIS seized large swaths of territory in both Syria and Iraq, it imposed a brutal form of governance based on its strict interpretation of Sharia law. The group's self-declared caliphate, which began in 2014, created a completely alternative state structure that displaced traditional governance and legal systems in the territories it controlled. ISIS not only operated as a military force but also as an authoritarian government, implementing harsh punishments, executing those who defied its rules, and enforcing its ideological vision with an iron fist. As a result, the lawlessness in areas under ISIS control was structured, albeit in an oppressive and violent manner. Its rise further alienated many Syrian civilians, as the group forced conformity through fear and violence, outlawing dissent and subjugating entire communities.

On the other side, pro-regime militias also proliferated in the wake of the regime's weakening control. The Assad government increasingly relied on paramilitary groups and loyalist forces to bolster its efforts. These militias were often formed along sectarian lines, with a particular focus on Shia and Alawite fighters. Groups like Liwa al-Quds, National Defense Forces (NDF), and other pro-regime militias grew in strength as they fought alongside the Syrian Army to retake rebel-held areas. Many of these militias operated outside the realm of official government forces, often engaging in abuses and war crimes with impunity. They were notorious for committing atrocities such as forced displacement, arbitrary executions, and the targeting of civilian populations. The NDF, for example, was involved in brutal campaigns to clear opposition-held areas and instill fear among civilians who dared to resist Assad's forces. The absence of any clear legal framework for these militias allowed them to operate unchecked, contributing to the widespread lawlessness in the country.

As the government's control over territory weakened and rival militias gained more power, the country descended further into chaos. These armed groups often clashed with each other over territory, resources, and power. The absence of a central authority or the rule of law meant that militias had the freedom to impose their own forms of governance, often using violence to settle disputes. In many areas, civilians had little choice but to comply with the demands of whichever group controlled their region, as militias used force to maintain dominance. These groups often set up their own checkpoints, extorted civilians for money or goods, and enforced their own arbitrary laws, creating a situation of constant fear and insecurity for ordinary Syrians.

The rise of militias also compounded the humanitarian crisis in Syria. As armed groups vied for control, they often cut off access to essential services like food, water, medical care, and education, exacerbating the suffering of the civilian population. In some cases, militias would prevent humanitarian aid from reaching opposition-held areas or seize supplies for their own use. This contributed to the widespread famine and disease that affected millions of Syrians. Furthermore, these militias were often responsible for targeting hospitals, schools, and civilian infrastructure, further reducing the resources available to the population. The situation became so dire that in many regions, civilians lived under siege, unable to escape the violence or access basic necessities.

In conclusion, the breakdown of government control and the rise of militias played a central role in the lawlessness and chaos that has characterized the Syrian civil war. With the state unable to maintain control over large parts of the country, various factions—both opposition and pro-regime—took matters into their own hands, creating a fragmented and dangerous landscape. The absence of the rule of law allowed militias to operate unchecked, further entrenching violence and instability. As the war continues, Syria remains trapped in a cycle of lawlessness, with multiple armed groups controlling various regions and no clear path to national unity or peace.

Chapter 8
The Struggle for Freedom

The Syrian civil war, which began as a peaceful movement for political change, quickly evolved into a brutal and bloody conflict, but at its core, it has always been a struggle for freedom. The peaceful protests that erupted in 2011 were driven by the hope for a more democratic, open, and just Syria. Ordinary citizens, including youth, intellectuals, and activists, took to the streets demanding an end to decades of authoritarian rule under the Assad regime. What began as a fight for freedom and human rights soon turned into a complex battle for survival as the regime responded with violent repression. The desire for freedom, however, remained the unifying theme for many who chose to resist, despite the overwhelming odds stacked against them.

As the conflict unfolded, the struggle for freedom became increasingly complicated, not only by the government's violent tactics but also by the rise of extremist factions, foreign interventions, and regional rivalries. The desire for a free Syria was hijacked by competing ideologies, as moderate opposition groups struggled to maintain their influence amid the growing strength of Islamist militias, including ISIS and al-Qaeda-linked forces. For many Syrians, the original goal of achieving a more democratic and free society became blurred as they found themselves fighting not only against the Assad regime but also against extremist ideologies that sought to impose their own rigid visions for Syria's future. The chaos of the conflict led to the fracturing of the opposition, but for those at the heart of the struggle, the pursuit of freedom was still central to their cause.

Despite the many challenges and betrayals along the way, the Syrian people's yearning for freedom persisted. Throughout the war, protests, uprisings, and acts of defiance continued, even in the face of overwhelming oppression. This chapter explores the ways in which Syrians—civilians, fighters, and activists—continued to push for their vision of a free Syria, battling against both internal tyranny and external forces. The struggle for freedom in Syria has been marked by incredible resilience, sacrifice, and a sense of hope, even as the path forward remains uncertain. Through the experiences of those who have fought for this cause, we see the enduring power of the human desire for liberty in the face of unimaginable adversity.

The Call for Democracy and Human Rights

The Syrian civil war, which began in 2011, was initially sparked by a call for political reform, democracy, and the respect of human rights. It was a movement rooted in the aspirations of ordinary Syrians who, after decades of authoritarian rule under the Assad family, sought a future in which they could express themselves freely, participate in the governance of their country, and live in a society that upheld the basic principles of justice, equality, and human dignity. The peaceful protests that first emerged were not just about ending the rule of Bashar al-Assad but about calling for systemic change: a transition to democracy that would respect the rights of all citizens, regardless of their religion, ethnicity, or political affiliation.

The demand for democracy and human rights was clearly articulated from the start, with protesters demanding the release of political prisoners, the lifting of emergency laws, and the establishment of a pluralistic political system. In the early months of the uprising, Syrians took to the streets across the country, in cities like Damascus, Homs, and Daraa, demanding an end to years of political repression and a more transparent, accountable government. Protesters were calling for the right to free speech, the right to hold free elections, and an end to the widespread corruption that permeated Syrian society. These calls for democracy were not just symbolic; they reflected the frustration and anger of a population that had long been denied basic freedoms, subjected to surveillance, torture, and arbitrary arrests by the regime's security forces.

However, the response from the Assad regime was swift and violent. Rather than addressing the legitimate grievances of the protesters, the government resorted to extreme measures, using live ammunition, tear gas, and arresting thousands of peaceful demonstrators. As the government cracked down, the call for democracy and human rights became a rallying cry for the opposition. While many initially joined the protests for political reforms, the regime's brutal response pushed more and more Syrians toward radicalized positions. The peaceful demonstrations, which had been intended as a call for political change, were met with violence, and this ultimately led to the militarization of the opposition. As government forces responded with lethal force, many defectors from the military, as well as civilians, formed armed groups to defend themselves and continue the struggle for democracy. This shift from peaceful protests to armed conflict marked a critical turning point in Syria's fight for freedom, but the core aspiration for human rights and democracy remained intact.

The struggle for democracy was complicated further by the rise of extremist factions that hijacked the revolution's original ideals. Groups like ISIS and Jabhat al-Nusra used the chaos of the civil war to impose their own vision of governance, which was grounded in authoritarianism, violence, and the strict application of their interpretation of Sharia law. The presence of such extremist groups posed a significant threat to the original ideals of democracy and human rights, creating a fractured opposition that was unable to unite under a single banner of reform. While the goal of overthrowing Assad's regime remained a priority, many Syrians who initially supported the revolution found themselves battling not only the government but also radical factions that undermined the cause of democracy and human rights.

Despite these challenges, the call for democracy continued to echo through Syria's towns, villages, and refugee camps. Activists, intellectuals, and members of civil society maintained their push for a Syria that would be inclusive, democratic, and just. These voices called for the recognition of the rights of minority groups, such as the Kurds, Christians, and Alawites, whose inclusion in a new political order was crucial to the future stability of Syria. They also emphasized the importance of addressing the humanitarian needs of millions of displaced Syrians and refugees, ensuring that the path toward democracy would be built on principles of equality, social justice, and the rule of law.

The international community, however, remained divided in its support for the Syrian opposition's calls for democracy. While Western countries, including the United States and European Union, voiced support for a political transition and the end of Assad's rule, their involvement was inconsistent, and often, strategic interests took precedence over the call for human rights. Some countries, including Russia and Iran, continued to back Assad, arguing that his government was the legitimate authority in Syria, and opposed foreign intervention. These divisions made it even more difficult for the Syrian people to achieve their goal of democracy, leaving them to continue their struggle largely without meaningful international support.

In conclusion, the call for democracy and human rights has remained a central tenet of the Syrian struggle, even as the war has evolved into a complex and multifaceted conflict. What began as a peaceful protest for political change quickly became a fight not only against the Assad regime but also against extremist ideologies that sought to impose authoritarian rule. Despite the overwhelming violence and the divisions within the opposition, the aspiration for a Syria that is democratic, inclusive, and respects human rights continues to be a guiding principle for many Syrians. The struggle for freedom in Syria is far from over, but the pursuit of democracy and human rights remains at the heart of the revolution that began in 2011.

The Syrian Opposition: A Fragmented Hope

The Syrian opposition, initially united in its demand for democratic reform and the removal of Bashar al-Assad's regime, quickly became fragmented as the conflict escalated. What began as a broad-based movement for political change, with peaceful protests and calls for greater freedoms, soon transformed into a highly divided and complex struggle. Internal divisions, ideological differences, external interventions, and the rise of extremist factions all contributed to the fragmentation of the opposition, making it difficult for the opposition to mount a coherent challenge to Assad's regime. The once unified hope for a democratic Syria was slowly undermined by competing visions, territorial control struggles, and foreign-backed factions, leaving the opposition in disarray.

At the start of the Syrian uprising in 2011, the opposition was relatively diverse, composed of secular and moderate groups, including activists, intellectuals, students, and defectors from the military. These groups were united by a common goal: to overthrow the Assad regime and establish a more democratic and inclusive Syria. The peaceful demonstrations that spread across the country reflected widespread popular discontent with decades of authoritarian rule, political repression, and corruption. Initially, the opposition was focused on nonviolent resistance, advocating for political reforms, civil liberties, and the establishment of a pluralistic political system. However, the Assad regime's violent crackdown on protesters in the early months of the uprising forced the opposition to take up arms, and the movement began to militarize.

As the conflict dragged on and the regime's brutal tactics continued to escalate, the opposition began to fragment along ideological, sectarian, and regional lines. Various rebel groups emerged, some of which were more moderate and secular, while others embraced a more Islamic vision for Syria's future. Groups like the Free Syrian Army (FSA), which initially represented the broader secular opposition, struggled to maintain unity as local militias and armed factions began to form in opposition-held areas. The FSA's lack of a centralized command structure and political agenda weakened its ability to coordinate military efforts effectively. This fragmentation deepened as more radical and Islamist factions, including groups like Jabhat al-Nusra (affiliated with al-Qaeda) and Ahrar al-Sham, gained prominence, especially after they began receiving substantial support from regional powers like Saudi Arabia, Qatar, and Turkey.

The rise of ISIS further complicated the opposition landscape. Originally an offshoot of al-Qaeda, ISIS capitalized on the chaos of the civil war to seize large areas of Syria and Iraq, declaring the establishment of a self-proclaimed caliphate in 2014. While ISIS initially garnered support from some rebel factions due to its military successes, its violent tactics, authoritarian rule, and rigid interpretation of Sharia law alienated many Syrians and rebel groups. The group's brutal treatment of civilians, its targeting of religious minorities, and its imposition of harsh laws made it a pariah even among opposition factions. As ISIS expanded its control over territory in eastern Syria, it created a new dynamic within the opposition, forcing groups to not only fight the Assad regime but also each other. The fragmentation of the opposition was now compounded by the rise of an extremist force that controlled vast swaths of territory and posed a direct threat to moderate factions.

The presence of foreign powers further exacerbated the divisions within the opposition. The Assad regime was heavily supported by Iran, Russia, and Hezbollah, which provided military aid, training, and logistical support. In contrast, various Western countries and Arab states backed the opposition, but their support was fragmented and inconsistent. The United States, while initially cautious, began providing military aid and support to Kurdish groups like the Syrian Democratic Forces (SDF), which became a key ally in the fight against ISIS. Meanwhile, Turkey focused on supporting opposition groups that were more aligned with Sunni Islamist ideologies, and Saudi Arabia and Qatar provided funding and weapons to factions such as Ahrar al-Sham. This external intervention created an environment where rebel groups aligned themselves with different foreign sponsors, often based on sectarian, ideological, or strategic considerations. This led to competing interests and a lack of cooperation among the various factions, making it difficult to form a unified front.

The lack of unity among the opposition also led to governance challenges in areas under their control. While the regime's control over Syria's major cities and infrastructure remained relatively strong, the opposition struggled to govern the areas they held. Local militias or rebel factions often set up their own administrations, sometimes with the backing of foreign powers. These local councils were often fragmented, inefficient, and unable to meet the basic needs of the civilian population. As rebel-held areas were besieged by both government forces and ISIS, the lack of a coordinated opposition leadership made it difficult to provide essential services such as healthcare, education, and food, exacerbating the humanitarian crisis.

In conclusion, the Syrian opposition, which once represented the hope for a democratic and inclusive future, became deeply fragmented over the course of the civil war. The ideological, sectarian, and regional divisions within the opposition, combined with the rise of extremist factions and external interventions, severely hindered their ability to unite and effectively challenge the Assad regime. The initial hope for a peaceful, democratic Syria was overtaken by infighting, radicalization, and the complexities of foreign involvement, leaving the opposition disoriented and weakened. As a result, the war has not only destroyed the fabric of Syrian society but has also made it nearly impossible for the opposition to present a unified alternative to the Assad regime, prolonging the conflict and deepening the suffering of the Syrian people.

Women in the Revolution: Agents of Change

Women have played a vital, though often overlooked, role in the Syrian revolution, both in the early days of peaceful protests and throughout the subsequent years of conflict. From the outset, women were at the forefront of the calls for political reform, human rights, and an end to decades of authoritarian rule under Bashar al-Assad. Their participation in the revolution, both on the streets and behind the scenes, challenged the traditional gender roles in Syrian society and made them agents of change in a deeply patriarchal environment. Despite the violence, repression, and marginalization they faced, Syrian women remained committed to the cause of freedom and democracy, contributing significantly to the movement in ways that continue to resonate in Syria's ongoing struggle for justice.

In the early days of the revolution, women were active participants in peaceful protests, which were predominantly composed of civilians from all walks of life. As protests spread across Syria in 2011, women from various backgrounds—including students, mothers, activists, and professionals—took to the streets demanding political reform and an end to the Assad regime's brutal policies. Women were involved in organizing protests, distributing pamphlets, and raising awareness about the repression they had long endured. For many women, the revolution represented an opportunity to break free from years of oppression and demand the same rights and freedoms as men. They became visible symbols of defiance in a country where women had been largely excluded from political life and public discourse. Prominent figures such as Razan Zaitouneh, a human rights lawyer, and Maya Naser, a journalist, became the faces of the revolution, showing that women could not only be participants but also leaders in the fight for change.

However, the Syrian government's violent response to the protests led to the militarization of the revolution and the fragmentation of opposition groups. As the war escalated, women's roles in the revolution evolved. While many continued to participate in protests and activism, others took on new roles in the conflict, such as fighters, medics, and human rights defenders. With the breakdown of state authority and the rise of local militias, women began to form their own organizations to support the revolution and help those affected by the war. In Kurdish-controlled areas, for example, YPG

(People's Defense Units) and YPJ (Women's Protection Units) emerged as key military forces fighting against both the Assad regime and ISIS. The YPJ, in particular, became symbolic of women's empowerment, as Kurdish women took up arms to defend their communities and fight for autonomy. These women, often motivated by a sense of justice and the desire to protect their families, embraced a form of resistance that defied both traditional gender norms and the violence of extremist forces.

Women also became deeply involved in the humanitarian aspects of the conflict. As the war displaced millions and caused widespread suffering, many women turned to community-based organizing, helping to provide basic needs like food, shelter, and medical care. Organizations led by women focused on addressing the specific needs of women and children in conflict zones, such as trauma counseling, reproductive healthcare, and protection from sexual violence. Women's rights activists played a crucial role in documenting human rights abuses and calling attention to the atrocities committed by both the regime and extremist groups. Despite facing personal risks, including imprisonment, torture, and death, many women bravely continued their activism, both within Syria and in exile, to ensure that the voices of the oppressed were heard.

However, the role of women in the revolution has not been without challenges. As the conflict intensified, women found themselves caught between competing forces—on one hand, the authoritarian regime, and on the other, radical Islamist factions like ISIS. While women's participation in the revolution initially sparked hope for greater gender equality and empowerment, many women faced the reality of being marginalized by both sides. In areas controlled by Islamist groups, women's rights were often severely restricted, with many being forced to adhere to strict interpretations of Sharia law. Women's participation in the military and activism was viewed with suspicion by some, and many were subjected to violence or abuse. In opposition-held territories, the absence of a strong centralized government and the rise of competing militias also created challenges for women's leadership roles, with some factions sidelining women's voices in favor of more traditional, male-dominated leadership.

Despite these obstacles, women's activism in Syria has been a powerful force for change. Women have not only fought for their own rights but have also worked to create a more inclusive and just society. Their involvement in the revolution has brought attention to issues of gender equality, human rights, and social justice, reshaping the political discourse in Syria. Women have been at the forefront of efforts to ensure that women's rights are included in any future political transition, advocating for equal representation in political negotiations and peace talks. They have worked to highlight the specific challenges women face in conflict, including sexual violence, forced displacement, and the loss of basic rights, and have pushed for international recognition of these issues.

In conclusion, women have been crucial agents of change in the Syrian revolution. From the earliest days of the uprising, Syrian women have played an active role in challenging the Assad regime and fighting for democracy, equality, and human rights. Their participation in the revolution, whether through protests, activism, or armed resistance, has reshaped the political landscape in Syria and challenged traditional gender norms. While women have faced immense challenges and marginalization, their resilience and determination have proven that they are not just victims of the conflict but powerful agents of change in the struggle for a better future for all Syrians.

Chapter 9
The Global Response

The Syrian civil war, which began in 2011, quickly escalated into one of the most devastating conflicts of the 21st century, drawing the attention of the international community and prompting various global powers to intervene in different ways. As the war intensified, the scale of the humanitarian crisis and the growing geopolitical stakes turned Syria into a focal point for international diplomacy, military intervention, and humanitarian aid. The global response to the conflict was marked by political and military support for different factions, humanitarian relief efforts, and deep divisions within the international community regarding the future of Syria and the Assad regime. Countries such as the United States, Russia, Iran, and Turkey, among others, became deeply involved, each pursuing their own strategic interests in the region.

Initially, many Western powers, including the United States and European Union members, called for an end to Assad's regime, condemning the regime's use of violence against civilians and supporting the opposition, both diplomatically and with non-lethal aid. However, as the conflict continued to deteriorate, the international response became increasingly fragmented. While some countries, such as the U.S. and certain European nations, pushed for sanctions and military action against the Assad government, others, like Russia and Iran, provided military and diplomatic support to preserve Assad's rule. These opposing positions, fueled by competing geopolitical interests, resulted in a complex and often contradictory international response that both exacerbated the conflict and prevented meaningful progress toward a resolution.

In addition to the direct military involvement by global powers, the war prompted one of the largest refugee crises in modern history. Neighboring countries such as Turkey, Lebanon, and Jordan bore the brunt of the displacement, with millions of Syrians fleeing the violence and seeking refuge across borders. The international community's response to this refugee crisis was mixed, with some countries providing substantial aid and resettlement opportunities, while others, particularly in Europe, struggled to manage the influx of refugees, leading to rising anti-immigrant sentiment. The failure to agree on a unified approach to Syria's refugees further complicated the global response and highlighted the broader challenges of international cooperation in addressing the aftermath of the conflict. The international community's approach to Syria remains one of the most complex and contentious aspects of the war, with no clear path forward toward a lasting peace.

The Role of the United Nations

The United Nations (UN) has played a significant, yet often contentious, role in addressing the Syrian conflict since its outbreak in 2011. As the war evolved into a major humanitarian crisis with severe political and geopolitical implications, the UN was called upon to provide humanitarian aid, mediate peace talks, and offer a platform for international dialogue. However, the organization's ability to effectively intervene and bring about a resolution to the conflict was severely limited by the complexities of the situation and the entrenched positions of the UN Security Council's permanent members, particularly Russia and China, who were steadfast in their support for the Assad regime.

One of the UN's primary roles in Syria has been providing humanitarian assistance. The conflict has caused widespread displacement, food insecurity, and the destruction of critical infrastructure. Millions of Syrians have depended on international aid for basic necessities such as food, shelter, clean water, and healthcare. The UN has coordinated humanitarian efforts through its agencies, including the World Food Programme (WFP), UNICEF, and the United Nations High Commissioner for Refugees (UNHCR), to deliver aid to affected populations both within Syria and in neighbouring countries that have taken in refugees. The UN has also provided support for the creation of refugee camps and worked to ensure that displaced Syrians have access to critical services such as medical care and education. However, delivering aid in such a volatile conflict environment has been challenging. Humanitarian convoys have been targeted, and the regime, opposition groups, and extremist factions have all at times blocked the delivery of aid for political and military reasons. The UN's ability to deliver aid was further hampered by a lack of security for aid workers and the complexities of navigating the many factions controlling different parts of Syria.

On the diplomatic front, the UN has worked through peace talks aimed at finding a political solution to the conflict. Early in the war, the UN Security Council (UNSC) attempted to broker ceasefires and push for political dialogue. The UN established the Geneva Process, which aimed to bring together the Assad government, opposition groups, and international stakeholders to negotiate a political settlement. However, these talks were repeatedly stalled due to the lack of cooperation from key parties and the rise of competing factions, particularly after the escalation of ISIS. Russia, as a key ally of Assad, has used its veto power in the UNSC to block resolutions that would have pressured the Syrian government, making it difficult for the UN to enforce any meaningful international pressure. While Western countries, including the U.S., have consistently called for Assad's removal, Russia and China have prevented UNSC resolutions that could have led to sanctions or military intervention against the regime, arguing that such measures would violate Syria's sovereignty. As a result, the UN's diplomatic efforts have been largely ineffective, and a political resolution to the conflict has remained elusive.

The UN Security Council (UNSC), composed of five permanent members with veto power (the U.S., Russia, China, the U.K., and France), has been a major impediment to meaningful action. Russia's support for Assad has been unwavering, and it has blocked any attempt by the UNSC to impose sanctions or authorize military intervention. In 2012, a Russian veto blocked a resolution that would have condemned the Syrian government's use of violence against civilians. This dynamic has resulted in a paralysis within the UNSC, where any resolution that would affect Assad's regime has been stymied by Russia's veto power. On the other hand, the West has pushed for stronger action against the Assad regime, including calls for military intervention and the imposition of a no-fly zone to prevent further government airstrikes on civilian populations. The lack of agreement on how to respond to the Syrian crisis has contributed to the perception of the UN as ineffective in resolving the conflict.

Additionally, the UN's peacekeeping role in Syria has been limited, largely because Syria's government has refused to allow international peacekeepers into the country. The United Nations Disengagement Observer Force (UNDOF) has operated in the Golan Heights, monitoring the ceasefire line between Syria and Israel, but it has not been deployed in areas of active conflict. Without the Syrian government's consent to allow international peacekeepers or a significant peacekeeping mandate, the UN's ability to enforce a peace settlement has been constrained. Furthermore, with the rise of multiple armed groups, including ISIS and Kurdish forces, the dynamics of the conflict became increasingly complex, making any peacekeeping mission extremely difficult to execute.

Despite these challenges, the UN has played a vital role in raising awareness of the Syrian crisis and generating international support for its resolution. Through its humanitarian missions and reporting, the UN has helped document war crimes and human rights abuses committed by all sides in the conflict. The United Nations Human Rights Council (UNHRC) has held investigations into the atrocities carried out during the war, while the International Criminal Court (ICC) has been urged to pursue accountability for crimes against humanity. The UN has also worked to ensure that the voices of the Syrian people are heard in international forums, highlighting the need for a political solution that respects Syria's sovereignty and upholds international law.

In conclusion, the UN has faced significant challenges in addressing the Syrian conflict, from delivering humanitarian aid to facilitating peace talks. Its ability to intervene effectively has been stymied by political gridlock within the UNSC and the complex nature of the war, including the involvement of multiple foreign powers and armed groups. However, the UN's humanitarian efforts and role in documenting war crimes have been crucial in mitigating some of the war's impacts, and its ongoing efforts remain an essential part of the global response to the crisis.

Sanctions and Diplomatic Efforts

The international community's response to the Syrian civil war has been marked by a combination of sanctions and diplomatic efforts, aimed at pressuring the Assad regime and seeking to find a resolution to the conflict. From the outset of the war in 2011, countries like the United States, the European Union, and various Arab League members imposed a range of sanctions targeting Syria's government and economy. These sanctions, intended to isolate the Assad regime politically and economically, aimed to force the government to cease its violent crackdown on protesters and eventually negotiate a political solution. Alongside sanctions, diplomatic efforts have been directed at facilitating peace talks, though these efforts have often been frustrated by geopolitical divisions, differing international priorities, and the regime's unwillingness to engage in meaningful negotiations.

Sanctions were among the first tools used by the international community in response to the Assad regime's brutal suppression of protests. The U.S. and the European Union imposed targeted sanctions aimed at the Syrian leadership, including travel bans, asset freezes, and restrictions on Syria's banking sector. These sanctions were designed to isolate President Bashar al-Assad and his inner circle, limiting their access to financial resources and foreign travel, as well as curtailing the regime's ability to access weapons and military equipment. Over time, sanctions were expanded to include sectors of the Syrian economy, such as oil, banking, and defense industries. For example, the U.S. imposed an oil embargo in 2011, effectively limiting Syria's ability to export oil, one of its most significant sources of revenue. The EU followed suit, prohibiting the import of Syrian oil and implementing economic measures aimed at curbing Assad's ability to fund his military operations.

Despite their intended impact, the effectiveness of sanctions in bringing about a change in Syria's government policies remains debated. While sanctions have undoubtedly strained the Syrian economy, contributing to hyperinflation, shortages of goods, and rising unemployment, they have not been successful in compelling Assad to step down or to change his approach to the opposition. The humanitarian impact of sanctions has been a point of contention, with critics arguing that the measures have disproportionately harmed the Syrian population rather than the regime itself. While sanctions targeted Syria's economic infrastructure and military capabilities, the regime's reliance on support from countries like Russia and Iran helped mitigate the economic pressure. Both Russia and Iran have continued to provide significant military and financial support to Assad, helping the government weather the impact of international sanctions and prolong the conflict.

Diplomatic efforts to resolve the Syrian conflict have been equally complicated, marked by an array of peace talks, international forums, and UN-sponsored negotiations, yet failing to achieve a lasting resolution. From 2012 onwards, the United Nations played a significant role in attempting to broker peace through the Geneva peace talks, with the goal of negotiating a political transition. These talks aimed to bring together representatives of the Syrian government, opposition groups, and international stakeholders to discuss a way forward. However, these negotiations have largely been unsuccessful due to the lack of a unified opposition and the regime's refusal to consider meaningful reforms or compromise. The Assad government's position, supported by its allies, remained that it would not relinquish power, insisting that any political settlement had to be based on preserving the status quo.

The Geneva Process was further complicated by the lack of coherence among the opposition factions. With the rise of extremist groups such as ISIS and al-Qaeda's affiliate Jabhat al-Nusra, the opposition became increasingly fragmented. The Syrian opposition groups, initially a diverse coalition of secularists and moderates, struggled to present a united front. This disunity was a key challenge for international mediators, as countries like the United States, Turkey, and Gulf Arab states supported different factions, while Russia and Iran backed the Assad regime. The international community was deeply divided over how to address the Assad regime, with some nations pushing for his removal, while others, particularly Russia and Iran, viewed him as a necessary ally for countering jihadist extremism in the region.

As the war continued, the Astana talks—initiated in 2017 by Russia, Turkey, and Iran—became another major diplomatic effort. Unlike the Geneva talks, the Astana process sought to focus on de-escalation zones and ceasefire agreements. The talks aimed to create a framework for political negotiations by stabilizing the military situation on the ground. However, the Astana process also faced significant challenges. The lack of input from the United States and other Western powers, as well as the continued involvement of jihadist groups and Syrian Kurdish forces, complicated efforts to find a solution that all parties could accept.

Furthermore, the UN's Security Council has been unable to agree on a coherent approach to the conflict due to the deep divisions between its permanent members. Russia, a key ally of the Assad regime, has consistently used its veto power to block UN resolutions aimed at imposing sanctions or taking stronger action against the regime. Meanwhile, the U.S. and its allies have pushed for more robust measures, including sanctions and the establishment of a no-fly zone, but these efforts have been stymied by Russia's intervention and support for Assad. This deadlock has contributed to the perception of the UN as ineffective in resolving the crisis, with conflicting interests among global powers making it difficult to reach a consensus.

In conclusion, the sanctions and diplomatic efforts surrounding the Syrian conflict have been pivotal in shaping the international response but have yielded mixed results. Sanctions have exerted pressure on the Syrian economy and military, but they have not been sufficient to bring about regime change or alter Assad's strategies. Diplomatic initiatives, such as the Geneva peace talks and Astana negotiations, have struggled to find a viable solution due to the fragmented opposition, the regime's entrenched position, and the lack of agreement among international actors. The failure of these efforts has contributed to the protraction of the conflict, leaving millions of Syrians caught in a war with no clear end in sight.

Humanitarian Aid: The Lifeline for Syrians

The Syrian civil war, now in its second decade, has resulted in one of the most devastating humanitarian crises of the 21st century. With over 500,000 people killed, millions displaced, and widespread destruction of homes, hospitals, schools, and infrastructure, Syrians have faced unimaginable hardships. In the face of these dire conditions, humanitarian aid has been a lifeline for many, offering critical support to civilians affected by the war. However, despite the best efforts of various international organizations, humanitarian aid has faced numerous obstacles, including access restrictions, violence, and political interference. As the war has dragged on, humanitarian aid has become an essential part of survival for millions of Syrians, providing food, medical care, shelter, and other basic necessities.

One of the primary organizations providing humanitarian assistance in Syria has been the United Nations (UN), along with its various specialized agencies, including the World Food Programme (WFP), UNICEF, and the United Nations High Commissioner for Refugees (UNHCR). The UN has coordinated a range of relief operations, providing food, clean water, shelter, healthcare, and education to millions of displaced Syrians. For example, the WFP has been distributing food to families in both government and opposition-controlled areas, while UNICEF has been working to provide education, immunizations, and psychological support to children who have been traumatized by the conflict. The UNHCR has focused on providing emergency shelter to displaced Syrians and helping refugees who have fled to neighboring countries like Turkey, Lebanon, and Jordan.

Despite these efforts, delivering humanitarian aid has proven to be a massive logistical challenge, especially as the war has become more fragmented. The Syrian government has repeatedly blocked or restricted aid delivery to opposition-held areas, particularly in places like Eastern Ghouta, Idlib, and Aleppo, where civilians have been trapped in besieged conditions for months or even years. The government has used access to aid as a bargaining chip, refusing to allow the UN or other humanitarian organizations into certain regions unless the opposition agrees to ceasefires or other political terms. This has left many civilians without access to essential supplies, exacerbating the suffering of populations already caught in the crossfire.

In addition to government restrictions, the rise of extremist groups, such as ISIS and Jabhat al-Nusra (al-Qaeda's affiliate in Syria), has further complicated aid efforts. These groups have controlled large swaths of territory at various points in the conflict and have often blocked or diverted aid, both for ideological reasons and to maintain control over populations in their areas. In areas like Raqqa and Mosul, ISIS imposed a brutal form of governance that restricted humanitarian access, and aid workers were often at risk of kidnapping, detention, or even execution. While many of these groups have been pushed back or defeated in recent years, their control over key areas of Syria continues to pose significant challenges to delivering aid to the most vulnerable populations.

The Russian and Iranian-backed Syrian government forces have also been accused of targeting humanitarian convoys, hospitals, and civilian infrastructure. Airstrikes by the Syrian military, often with Russian support, have destroyed vital facilities, including hospitals and medical centers that were crucial for providing care to the wounded and sick. The use of siege tactics by government forces has also made it difficult for aid to reach besieged cities and towns, resulting in starvation and disease. In addition, the government's practice of using humanitarian aid for political leverage has resulted in many aid deliveries being disrupted or delayed. Civilians living under siege conditions have often been forced to rely on illicit smuggling networks for basic necessities, which is neither safe nor sustainable.

Cross-border aid has been another critical avenue for providing relief to Syrians, particularly in opposition-controlled areas and refugee camps outside Syria. Turkey, Jordan, and Lebanon have all played important roles in providing shelter and support for Syrian refugees. These countries have hosted millions of Syrians fleeing violence, and many international organizations have used these countries as staging points for delivering aid into Syria. The cross-border humanitarian aid mechanism was set up by the United Nations to allow aid to be sent from Turkey and Jordan into Syria without needing the Syrian government's permission. However, this mechanism has been contested by Russia and Syria, which have argued that it violates Syria's sovereignty. In 2020, the UN Security Council voted to reduce cross-border aid operations, further limiting access to critical supplies.

The local response to the crisis, including grassroots organizations and volunteers, has also been essential in filling the gaps left by international aid efforts. Local groups, including the White Helmets (Syria Civil Defence), have been critical in providing rescue operations, evacuations, and medical care in areas that are hard to reach due to ongoing military operations. These local actors, often working in dangerous conditions, have provided hope and support to thousands of Syrians in the most devastated regions.

Despite the obstacles, humanitarian aid has undoubtedly saved countless lives and alleviated some of the suffering caused by the war. However, the scale of the humanitarian crisis remains overwhelming, and ongoing conflicts, political divisions, and logistical challenges continue to hamper relief efforts. The need for political solutions to ensure better access to aid, greater cooperation from all parties involved, and sustainable development will be critical to Syria's recovery in the years to come. Without sustained international support and a resolution to the conflict, the humanitarian situation in Syria will continue to remain dire, and aid will remain a vital lifeline for millions of Syrians.

Conclusion

The Syrian civil war has left a profound and indelible mark on Syria, the Middle East, and the world. What began as a peaceful uprising against a brutal authoritarian regime has escalated into a devastating conflict, marked by staggering loss of life, widespread displacement, and the near-total destruction of Syria's infrastructure. Through the course of this war, Syria has gone from a unified state to a fragmented battleground, where multiple factions, foreign powers, and local militias vie for control, all while the Syrian people endure unimaginable suffering.

The road to peace in Syria has been obstructed by complex, overlapping interests, both internal and external. The role of foreign intervention—whether through military support for the Assad regime, assistance to various opposition groups, or the fight against extremist factions—has played a pivotal role in prolonging the conflict. At the same time, the strategic, ideological, and sectarian divides within Syria itself have compounded the challenges of achieving a political resolution. The rise of extremist groups like ISIS, competing visions of Syria's future, and the fractured nature of the opposition have made it exceedingly difficult to unite the country under a shared vision of peace and democracy.

For the Syrian people, the war has not only been a fight for survival but a struggle for dignity, human rights, and freedom. Throughout the conflict, ordinary Syrians have shown incredible resilience and courage, fighting not only against the regime but also against the extremist forces that have sought to impose their own version of governance. From the women who took up arms to protect their families and communities, to the activists who risked their lives to document atrocities and call for justice, to the millions who have been displaced and have endured unimaginable hardship, the Syrian people's hope for a better, freer future has been one of the defining features of this war.

The global response to Syria's plight has been fragmented and inconsistent, with humanitarian aid efforts, sanctions, and diplomatic initiatives all playing their parts, yet failing to end the war or bring lasting peace. While international humanitarian organizations have saved countless lives, political solutions have remained elusive, largely due to the competing interests of global and regional powers. The United Nations, despite its significant efforts, has struggled to enforce meaningful peace initiatives due to the political gridlock within the Security Council, and the failure of peace talks has left Syrians with little hope of a resolution. Instead, the international community has largely reacted to the humanitarian crisis and the rise of extremism, rather than addressing the root causes of the conflict.

Ultimately, the destruction of the Syrian state, the collapse of infrastructure, the rise of militias, and the growing sectarian divisions have created a complex and fractured society where the path to recovery seems increasingly distant. The Syrian war is not just a crisis in the conventional sense, but a deep wound in the heart of the Middle East, with long-lasting consequences that will likely be felt for generations. Rebuilding Syria will require more than just physical reconstruction; it will require the healing of the social, political, and economic divisions that have torn the country apart.

As Syria moves forward, it is critical that any lasting peace deal takes into account the voices of the people, and their desire for a society where human rights, freedom, and democracy can thrive.

True peace will only come when Syrians are able to reclaim their country from the violence and trauma of the last decade and build a new Syria that is inclusive, just, and free from the authoritarianism and extremism that have marked its recent past.

In conclusion, the Syrian civil war has been a conflict of unprecedented complexity, where the struggle for freedom, democracy, and human rights collided with entrenched power, foreign intervention, and the rise of extremism. Though the road to peace is long and fraught with obstacles, the enduring resilience of the Syrian people remains a powerful testament to the human spirit's ability to withstand unimaginable hardship. As the world watches, the ultimate question remains: Will Syria rise from the ashes, or will it continue to be consumed by the forces of division and violence? The answer lies not just in military victories or political negotiations, but in the hearts and minds of the Syrian people who continue to dream of a better, peaceful future.